Bogdan A. Papadie

The Brotherhood of spies

Volume 1

Copyright © by **Bogdan A. Papadie** 2016

Text adaptation © *by* **Horia Cocos**

CONTENTS

WARNING

The present volume is but the first in a series dedicated to the actions of the secret services. Organizations more often than not behind the consequential events that had left their mark on world history, the latest of which, namely the bloody terrorist attacks in Paris, Brussels, Istanbul and Nice, being but the exception that proves the rule. Though I am not a conspiracy buff, I can by no means deny the evidence: behind the convulsions that have rocked Europe in the last 12 years there lies a genuine cobweb woven by the secret services! Secret services that wage a tooth and nail war for European and world domination.

Truth or fiction? Attempting to set them apart I realized that the aforementioned terrorist attacks could not have been carried out in want of some entities having the logistical potential required for covert top level operations. Someone must be at least gullible to give credence to the idea of young Islamists having the data and logistical potential needed to penetrate and deceive vast intelligence structures (for instance, France has 33 secret services), all exquisitely financed and equipped, as nobody can provide a logical explanation of more than 2 millions "third world" migrants having been allowed to wander freely through an European Union that had invested billions of Euros to secure its borders. Hence a relevant bafflement: *who and why had made possible such deeds that had left a trail of blood and grief all over the world and what role the espionage had played in this evil scenario?*

Before beginning to read this book, let⊠s try to answer briefly a question: What the espionage is? As far as I am concerned, espionage is the black art of international relations. For seven millenniums, espionage had been pigeonholed among the black arts of history, clearly set apart from the political affairs. Only in the France of the XVII century the cardinals Richelieu and Mazarin – each of them holding the office of Prime Minister for 18 years – usher formally the espionage into the political alcove, Mazarin being behind a famous assertion still in fashion today: *The espionage is a night lamp shedding light over the gloomy paths of politics.*

Both espionage and counterespionage are all-knowing, all-powerful and ubiquitous. They miss nothing, not even people⊠s private lives. And in particular their weaknesses, sins, passions, penchants, intellectual potentials, the diseases afflicting them, phobias and wishes, the black spots lingering in their past. Absolutely everything! And are we then supposed to believe they cannot thwart by knowledge the deeds of some fanatics fancying themselves as martyrs?

Not few times did I hear that the success ratio of terrorist attacks is underpinned by their lack of predictability. I do not deny, people can be aggressive, evil or charming, desperate, good-natured, reckless, daring or greedy, free-handed or despicable; they can be nitpickers, vain, covetous or dissolute, fanatics or hypocritical; they can turn possessive, humble, cheap or boastful, depraved, liars, gluttonous or keen. But all these concealed character traits can make up as many priceless data used mainly for recruiting, "blind exploiting," compromising, blackmailing, directing, manipulating or influencing them. When in charge of the French counterespionage service, count de Marenches had declared at a press conference: *Nowadays, in order to rule as many people as possible, not the territories but the souls of those people are conquered. Once you have the soul you have the man; and when you have the man the territory comes by itself.*

I let you draw the conclusions…

THE AUTHOR

THE UNSEEN SHADOW

From the times of old people have entertained and will always entertain all sorts of delusions. Some more terrible than the others. Some aim to order diversity, others to diversify unity, and the heavyweights of the world – some carefully hidden, others in plain sight but still hidden nevertheless – want to tailor it to their own interests, to master everything living in the world. It is not so hard to accomplish a goal since it was already proved that the entity controlling the money nurtures the perfect delusion of being able to do whatever it wants with this world and any other of the visible, invisible, or predictable worlds out there. It can trigger crises and wars, indebt and wreck whole states, control the controlling and undermine the undermining itself (not with a view to negate the negation but to double it!), despite still being around a wisely crafted saying about that drawing the sword perishing by the sword.

The quite troubling question still asked – and probably further asked more and more bluntly, on the mysteries of some shadows that had cast and still cast light into the minds of the decision makers, is an essential one: *How much darkness and light those shadows cast?* And other questions consequently popping up: *Where is the sun bringing them to life? What heavens does this go up in? And who is still eyeing it?*

The book here delves into those shadows and reveals flash like as much as it can be revealed of their dramas and mysteries.

There is an ongoing war of this world, a war either thought, security, world or life wouldn't be without. This war is known as *knowledge*. And knowledge means incorporated information, namely removed indetermination. Man is nothing but a cognitive concept grounded mainly on this monad of the cognitive universe: *information*. Though this line of reasoning is straightforward, it will always look extremely intricate and complex. Certainly, man is or looks like being only substance, energy and information. But only God knows whether or not there is something beyond! The three states of the same condition do not separate but integrate each other. They can exist but together, each of them being vital for the others and even for itself. One single minute of lapsed information would spell death to man!

The information services are the sensors, eyes, ears, analyzers and synthesizers of the human being's, society's, security's and life's universal monad, known, as aforementioned, as information. When added on information is the brick of knowledge. And in the act of construction brick means value. This doesn't lead to the information services encompassing everything, that in want of them there would be neither common men, nor scholars and nor donkeys, the latter making to one of the most sensitive and consequential categories which Napoleon had been ordering during battles to be provided the best protection by deploying them in the middle of formation. It leads only to the conclusion that for the policy makers throwing themselves into the universal battle for power and survival, the information services acquire data and almost all the other elements information is extracted, synthesized, and if appropriately detailed, from. In want of this information there is no viable decision, nor power, nor influence, nor survival. Without eyes man is blind, without mind is an animal.

By and large that is what the information services are doing. They take in from and take out to the world what they call – "intelligence." "Intelligence" doesn�t mean an institution but a concept. Or maybe an institution of a concept. It is what Michelangelo said a statue was: a preexistent shape in stone which the sculptor identifies and takes out thence to offer to the people�s eyes. Because down there inside the raw stone he is the only one to see it. The same with the information. The process whereby the information is extracted from the mountain of data, images, phrases, sentences, words and everything said, seen, heard is called *intelligence*, being both a science, protracted experience, namely a practice – and most important – an art. A strategic art. Because information, even that at the ground, tactical level, always bears a strategic value.

As previously said, in a fractal technique based approach there are brought to light, as few have done before, some truths which in our society teeming with deceptions and stratagems are seldom exposed without sparking gut reactions on behalf of those getting the things harder, or better said by no means willing to understand what it is all about.

The author shows that during history and in the entire systems almost all are going into... *political police*, hereby meaning the whole multiphase checkered or frequency leap measures called on to defend more or less directly, more or less strategically (as a rule offensive or anyway exceedingly active) a political regime against another political regime, or rather against all those disliking it, regardless how democrats or autocrats would they fancy themselves being, regardless what color would they pretend to belong to. Red, green, yellow, blue, orange or mingled, let alone the infinite combinations among them.

Therefore, the first rule inside an area with neither rules nor irregularities: *all are going into political police!* The author doesn⊡t beat about the bush, looks for no euphemisms, but minces not his words as befitting a writer.

The second rule of a strict and badass "Intelligence:" *all the information services are breaking the law!* There are no legal spies around!

The New World Order within an international system still relying on states boils down after all to a cunning, mastery, terrorist, strategic and relentless attempt of a occult elite to form a world government and gain access to absolute power by any conceivable means, in particular the super-financial ones.

That mankind is heading, like it or not, to some kind of a world governance looks like an outcome not only obvious but likewise possible, and taking into account the future of a technological culture and a living based on Internet, even necessary. But a power thirsty occult elite when attempting to skip the necessary stages in the building of a long lasting structure, is not only triggering a devastating seismic effect but can generate – and it really does it! – a humongous chaos akin to the economic and financial crises that had rocked and still rock the world, and to some kind of never ending world war which breaks out catastrophically every now and then.

The apocalypse and masonry conspiracy, the Fourth Reich... sound like fairy tales. But they are not fairy tales. They have a clue, as like seen in a fabulously amplified 3D action.

Wells, the open conspiracy, to be sinarchist, namely directed by the Great Masters of Ascension to lay ground for the second coming of Christ. The Great White Brotherhood, its inner esoteric plan to overlook the passing to a new world order (NOM), etc, etc.

The Fourth Reich expression is employed by the conspiracy theorists. Not to stand out of the crowd but to look more menacing through their invisibility... A supposed world governance would be at the beck and call of fascists and

Jews… That⍰s what they mean. To all these theories flooding the web pages there could be added those of Extraterrestrials and Intraterrestrials. To have everything turned upside down…

Coup d⍰état, black choppers, advertising consumption, Cabalists, Cathars, Templar Knights, Rosicrucians, Freemasons, Illuminatis, etc… they all bring to life a New World Order through a "New Age" religion, the imperial worship of Antichrist.

No matter how strange or frightening and phantasmagoric these words might look like we all know they exist not only on real and virtual pages but likewise into the heads of some people seeing themselves as the absolute masters of all the worlds…

Some of the genuine supports of these fancies are part and parcel of the manipulating techniques and mind controlling ones, all as real as could be, others rely on the boundless gluttony (to be found in various degrees within each two legged human eating the bread of idleness on Earth!)…

Pope Benedict XVI said that behind the world economic collapse was the profit frame of mind.

…Profit, consumerism, never ending indebting of each of us, new forms of slavery, the eternal dependence on banks and illiterate elites (the only culture these shadow elites having a soft spot for being that of money), consumer-man, indebted-man, dependent-man, good for nothing-man…

What is the role the secret services are playing in this insame struggle for power and world domination? Just now have the secret services got involved or are they doing this ever since there are people, interests and the power to fight for around? The answer is as straightforward as it can be: Where there is a man there is a mean thought, one good and a dubious third one. When there are two people there are two good thoughts, two mean thoughts, two dubious ones and two primary spies, witty and bent on doing wrong. Where there are seven billion people there are seven billion suspects, seven billion spies, 14 billion eyes and 14 billion cerebral hemispheres seeking, seeking and keeping on seeking… Ecce Homo!

The author shuns this maze. But he can⌐t shake it off. That who had read *Arthashastra*, penned by the Indian Kotylio – monumental work of antiquity in several volumes – or but those 30 pages of Sun Tzi⌐s The Art of War, has already learned that the ancient people were spying on each other as much as our contemporaries, while the Greeks entertained no second thoughts about using a Trojan Horse to cheat their way inside the walled Troy… The "clues" comprised inside these two seminal works of antiquity turned into real directories even for nowadays spies…

The author pens several lines on Lysander, the leader of Spartans, who had been using on that time an early form of secret writing on wax encased wooden plates...

In the Roman Empire there was a secret police, "Frumentarii," acting also as a censoring agency. The Romans were highly skilled at political manipulations, espionage and dirty operations. The word terrorist comes from *terror-terroris*, much used in the Roman legions practice to subdue the conquered populations through fear and terror. All the world powers are well trained in doing this. There is no power without information, no information without espionage, no espionage without breaking the law...

Hannibal was also relying on data acquiring. The Roman spies had found the place Nicomedia had been hiding in and had him commit suicide.

Both Decebal, the king of the antique Dacia, and Caesar were employing spies and lurkers. Decebal's spy, whose name is known to us – Atticus – made it to the Roman Senate. It would be interesting to learn how many members of the present Parliaments are on the payroll of foreign information services.

Each of the Roman legions during the reign of Caesar was comprising 10 spies and lurkers. Some were working for Caesar while the others, his faithful Brutus included, for someone else... Caesar had even made up a spy alphabet based on letter substitution.

Theodora was in charge of the Byzantine espionage, its spies having saved the throne of Justinian. The Catholic Church, as thoroughly proven, couldn◻t but have in its turn a large spy network.

"Gentleman spy" is a concept used by the Englishmen. Meaning that most of the British spies were coming from cultural environments. Pierre Alamire (1470 – 1536), composer, engineer, diplomat and spy is a telltale example. Like the great painter Peter Paul Rubens (1577 – 1640) who had acted also as a secret messenger.

*

Somewhere in the midst of this volume the author writes: *On the Kahlenberg rise close by Vienna there had been set an inscription bearing the following text: To the memory of the Romanian soldiers who in the year 1683, during the siege of Vienna, had their share of contribution to the relief of the city. Nurturing the hope to shake off the High Porte sovereignty but unable to get plainly involved in the battles, the Prince of Wallachia (historic province of Romania), Serban Cantacuzino (1678 – 1688), and that of Moldavia (another historic province of Romania), Gheorghe Duca, picked the path of informative approaches, espionage and even sabotage (replacing the guns◻ shots with straws), acting as "double agents," to use a modern terminology. Thus, Serban Cantacuzino had mediated both the movement of the Imperial couriers and that of the information, letting the Austrians know in due time the Turks had run short of the resources needed to carry on the siege.*

(...) The High Steward Constantin Cantacuzino (1655 – 1716) had been one of the scholars of that time who had taken up informative actions, becoming the man in charge of what could be seen as the first service of this kind in the Romanian Provinces, the present day Romania. Among the activities taking place at the Secret Chancery there could be included: receiving agents bringing information from other countries, editing, translating and "opening" the secret correspondence. As a matter of fact, the High Steward had also made up a "cipher." The Palace at Mogosoaia (near Bucharest – the capital city of Romania) was more often than not hosting secret meetings with foreign envoys, sometimes under guise, later on being directed to leave on secret paths. An exquisite skill of the Great Steward was that of worming out information from foreign interlocutors without them realizing that, in particular during feasts wine was lavishly provided to the guest (...)

In other words "blind exploitation" is a procedure well known from times long gone, the prowess of "worming out information" being referred to since antiquity.

*

If talking about the Romanian Provinces, let's remind the way Grigore I Ghica (1660 – 1664) had appointed Nicolae Milescu Spatarul (1636 – 1708) diplomatic agent (capuchehaie) at the High Ottoman Porte. Milescu had acted as influence agent for the former prince Gheorghe Stefan. He got used to the ways of "the diplomatic espionage" at manifold European courts. These had been probably the reasons why upon the recommendation of Dosithei, the Patriarch of Jerusalem, Milescu had been admitted among the courtiers of the Tzar of Russian, Aleksei Mihailovici, who would dispatch him on a secret mission to China to pick up information and establish confidential political relations or, as specified in the mandate (imperial ukase) handed to him, "*to undertake researches, employing any suitable means, among all those in the know and find out the genuine truth.*" (…)

*

The fact that the Romanian Provinces had been of interest for the European powers is proven by the presence here of some agents. Among others we talk about Matteo Murano (? – 1503), physician, but in fact agent for Venice, who had arrived in August 1502 at the court of Stefan cel Mare (Stephen the Great) to provide medical treatment for the prince of Moldavia. Some medieval sources make clear reference to the Moldavian great prince having been assassinated by Murano through the use of a poisoned "miraculous" ointment. The order would have been issued straight from the highest hierarchy of the Catholic Church after the assurances given by the Great Stefan to the Ottoman Porte about him not interfering anymore in a future conflict between Christians and Turks. Reason why "the Champion of Christendom" of yesteryear turns public enemy number one for Vatican. (…)

*

The informative, spying activity carried out by the Habsburg Empire in the Balkans steps up and grows better organized with the 1782 establishment of diplomatic agencies. Both the Austrians consuls and other Great Powers◻ were conveying valuable data, in particular over the intentions of the Ottoman Empire, acquired by means of an informant network in the Romanian Provinces, Serbia and Bulgaria. For instance, in March 1794, the "commercial" agent Markelius writes to the Austrian Chancellor, Kaunitz, about "the money needed to pay our agents."

But in the Balkans were also operating agents both of Prussia and England, these turning thus into consequential spots on the map of "the secret war," as they would stay so during the following centuries.

*

The author gleans important information out of the world of those going in for this shady war of the shadows of any kind. There are not missing William Moorcroft (1767 – 1825), seen as blazing a trail in the knowledge of Mount Himalaya, and Francis Younghusband (1863 – 1912), playing an important role in the exploration of the roads to India and

China. Deemed as one of the most capable spies England had had in the XIX century, Francis Richard Burton (1821 – 1890) was at the same time both an exquisite explorer and man of science in Middle East and Africa, having also translated the fairy tales collection from "One Thousand and One Nights."

The author refers to the French Deuxième Bureau, to the Dreyfus Affair, to Louise de Keroualle (1649 – 1734), seen as "the best known of the French spy women" from the XVII century, to the agent activity of the "disguised spy" Charles Éon de Beaumont (1728 – 1810), agent of the royal secret service ("Secret du roi") in Russia and England, to the Napoleon⁇s army of spies, to the 10.000 German spies, among whom was Johann Gotfried Brügemann, too, (1750 – 1802), who had stolen the secret of the loom from England, but also to baroness Kaulla (1850 – 1910), who became mistress of the France Minister of Defense…

Benjamin Franklin (1706 – 1790) was himself a spy… The American women unionist agents, the agents of the Romanian prince Alexandru Ioan Cuza, "Operation Briefcase," the betrayal of the Romanian Prime Minister Titu Maiorescu… "Military Intelligence" (MI5) established in 1909, the Royal Castle Peles (Sinaia/Romania) turned into a meeting place for the agents connected to the officers from Austria Hungary, who had carried out reconnaissance missions in the Carpathian Mountains… Sidney George Reilly (1874 – 1925) the most important British agent in

Russia, "Deutschland über alles und Mata Hari" the "Soviet man" Jack London… the atomic spies, Richard Sorge, double agents, etc, etc.

The author doesn⍰t overlook any of the pivotal moments of the great battles waged in the shadow of knowledge, in the antechambers of the momentous decisions that had changed the world and would probably take it in the end either to doomsday or to a new resurrection. The management of information is harsh, spectacular, but nonetheless a never ending necessity. Here there⍰s neither mercy nor compassion, but fight only. That⍰s why the secret services all over the world, though under parliamentary and other state institutions control are in fact given the green light to do whatever they think necessary. They cannot be confined because there are no confines in the field of information. It⍰s a delusion to believe you can keep under control those bringing from the deepest shadows shards of light assisting the power in seeing, understanding, being. By wishing to keep the spies under control regardless of consequences means to cut your own throat, to throw willingly dirt into your own eyes. The life of the spies and of all the others working in the field of information is important as long as it provide information. That⍰s why the world of spies is mastered by rules like no others in the daily life. To write about such kind of life – even if having an intimate knowledge of its – means always running a significant risk. The risk of not knowing what are you talking about. But it also incurs an important benefit, when and only when you know what are you writing about. A situation befitting the author of this volume on the shadow of the shadow war, author knowing what is he writing about.

Brigade General (r) **Gheorghe Vaduva**

INSTEAD OF INTRODUCTION

The book here is a sketch of the world espionage history and of the redeployment of the forces involved in time in secret confrontations. It is, by your allowance, an introduction in the secretive world of espionage, needed for a better understanding of the facts and decisions of those involved in many an event that bore influence in some way or other on human universal history.

History now rewritten by way of reshaping the spheres of influence. We see an increasing assertive Russia and a European Union institution[1] under a rising tide of disproval right in the countries that had laid its foundation. In Germany, France, Italy, Spain, Greece, Great Britain, Sweden, Austria, the undercurrents standing against the European Union institution gain more and more strength. Among other things, there come under attack the single currency, the cumbersome bureaucracy and the lack of responsibility as to the man on the street, the rising unemployment, the disappearance of manufacturing industries, the falling standards of education, the increasing age of retirement, the uncontrolled immigration and the overwhelming of the local population by foreigners sharing no values whatsoever with Europe and its traditions, the moral degeneration and the dictatorship of political correctness.

On its own turf the European Union is struggling to survive, the daily life conditions being way more convincing that both a system press and a host of "political analysts" spreading for decades mendacious visions. The Euroskeptics of any feather, ranging from nationalistic patriots to the economically driven centrists and up to the radical left are gaining more and more votes in almost all of the countries in the western and central Europe. A gloomy reality of the present times foretelling the collapse of the United Europe or the end result of a huge espionage and disinformation operation masterminded by the United States?

World consequential political analysts, first of all the American ones, from reputable academic institutions, back and lay blame of this anti European conspiracy in the last two decades mostly on the Washington policy, on this policy being carried out by the ultra-conservative circles closely associated to the interests of the military industrial complex in the United States. Worth noticing, from 1990 onward the United States have continued on and on an arms race that in the end led to a great military imbalance between USA and the rest of the world. Nonetheless, the economic boom of Germany occurring despite economic crises and the flood of Syrian refugees, as well as the major investments of the main European powers in developing the community arsenal, couldn't go unnoticed by the Americans.

Obviously, the White House could not tolerate a strong economically and militarily European Union, as it looks awry to a possible closer rapprochement between Union and

Russia, a country bearing huge mineral and energetic resources, with an increasingly stronger army and a well developed informative system. As many reasons to notice, according to the renowned writer and political military analyst Colonel (r) Florian Garz, in the foreign policy American political discourse a series of expressions meant to incur bafflement and inquietude: *Resorting to war as a way to maintain peace* (possibly the greatest nonsense in the history); *The exclusive right of USA to unleash preventive wars*, the first being that waged on Iraq; *Crusade against terrorism* – perceived in the entirety of the Muslim states as a "crusade against Islam;" *Those not on our side are against us*; *the last destination of the world history is the American society; USA the nation world cannot do without.*

More worrisome than anything else is the Washington⊠s pretence that the United States, as the "only superpower" is entitled through its historically unprecedented military might to shape by its own will a new world political order. In another words, the USA hegemony on the world is unavoidable, indispensable and mandatory. Nevertheless, most of the responsible and unbiased political analysts believe that mankind is heading not for an Americanized "unipolar world" but for a "multipolar world." The latter process will be a long and painful one.

The globalization process is rendered utterly dissimilarly on the two shores of the Atlantic Ocean. The European Union delineates itself more and more as a power apart from the

United States of America. At the onset of 2004, for the first time in its history, the European Union had adopted a security strategy of its own sharing but few common features with both the Unites States◻ security strategy and NATO◻s[2], which as a matter of fact has not been working for years on end. More and more people are convinced that Washington is using "the war against terrorism" as a cover up for the military conquering of oil rich strategic areas and other valuable natural resources. In a nutshell, the ultra-conservative leading political circles from Washington wish to turn the American military supremacy into global economic advantages.

Do the Europeans witness this helplessly? Not in the least! However, they are making a huge mistake by attempting to sideline Russia. Instead of attracting Moscow to a union sweeping from Atlantic Ocean to the far away Asian steppes and from the Mediterranean Sea up to the Arctic Ocean, the European Union is playing unwillingly into the hands of the United States. Right the global power that had triggered the great economic crisis and the severe issues related to the single currency, deficiencies that had undermined and still undermine the United Europe. A Europe that morphed into an empire interested way too much into conquering new spheres of influence to conceal its endeavors to encircle Russia according to the "Anaconda" strategy, devised for the first time in the early XX century by the Briton Halford Mackinder[3]. Trough this strategy, the Europe Asia space is slowly but surely strangled by the "unionists" through limiting the Russia⬚s access to the "open" seas.

The same "Anaconda" strategy is the argument explaining most of the geopolitical movements of the last two and a half decades:

- the invitation made, even formally, by the American state secretary John Kerry[4] in the summer of 2013 to Georgia[5] – a state with a negligible economy, weakened by internal conflicts and comprising two hostile regions went out of control, South Ossetia[6] and Abkhazia[7] – to join NATO. In this case, an extra strategic argument is the undermining of the Russia – Iran relation, and the total encirclement of Iran on every hand: East – Afghanistan, Pakistan; South – Saudi Arabia, the Gulf countries[8]; West – Turkey, Iraq; North – Georgia.

- the invitation made to the Moldova Republic[9] to join the North Atlantic Pact – a country encountering the same severe economic problems as Georgia, and with the rebellious provinces of Transnistria[10] and Gagauzia[11]. This movement is aimed to cut off for good the Russia⬚s access to the Danube "Mouths,"[12] an overwhelmingly important geostrategic area (location where Danube flows into the Black Sea[13], providing *four strategic openings*: one to the Black Sea, other to a ground road, the end or beginning of a transport route to the North through Ukraine or to the East toward Russia, another fluvial route to the heart of Europe and further on to the "cold" seas; and an immediate ground opening toward the Balkan region[14].

- the Deveselu shield[15] – the preposterous "argument" of taking down the "Iranian nuclear tipped missiles" aimed toward Europe, having president Putin burst in laughter during a TV interview, turns groundless even for laymen against the background of the late negotiations;

- the American Chinese conflict over the Air Identification Zone announced by China (ADIZ – East China Sea);

Moreover, the European Union mainly assisted breaking out of the Ukraine crisis does not arise accidentally shortly after the headways the Russian diplomacy over Syria and Iran had made. The possible avoiding by means of the Russia mediation, even for the near future only, of a large scale regional war with consequences hard to assess seems not to be liked by all the sides involved. The reaction consisted in moving the action area closer to Russia, seen as the main party standing against the present hegemonic Euro Atlantic system. Hence and up to the Moscow reaction there was but a simple step to take, and the result of the Russian secret services☐ representatives assault wasn☐t long in appearing. Ukraine had initially grown reluctant as to the European Union by refusing to sign the Association Accord[16] (A.A) and the Comprehensive Free Exchange Accord[17] (ALSAC) with EU at the Vilnius summit[18], while adhering instead to the Russia Belarus Kazakhstan Custom Union[19] (UVRBK). Later on the conflict that had led to the retrocession of the

Crimea peninsula[20] and the hybrid war in the eastern Ukraine had broken out.

Through the previously taken movements the Russian Federation had proved its willingness to resort to compulsory measures, thinly veiled threats and preemptive sanctions – ill ominous actions for the envisaged Europe Asia Union[21] (a regional integration concept devised by Moscow). Furthermore, it is proved once again that the extra economic pressures so much called on previously are long gone in Europe. And EU still lags behind USA over a coherent foreign policy. Instead, the European Union is one of the main global economic players, unlike Russia which marred by an under par economy has a very coherent and performing foreign policy.

Back to the issue, since it could not turn a blind eye to the fate of those about 10 millions Russians in Ukraine, Russia had to choose between providing assistance to an independent Ukraine in its entirety or getting officially involved in the ethnic conflicts simmering throughout the neighboring country. But an open involvement meant falling right in the trap set by its enemies while watching idle to the events taking place in its close vicinity was tantamount to giving up the status of great power. Therefore, this dilemma had but three solutions:

- saving the Ukraine integrity against the background of a friendly independence toward Moscow (what Russia had failed to achieve);

- official splitting of Ukraine over hard to devise ethnic and linguistic separation lines, a project hard to bring to life without a Bosnia[22] scenario any peace seeking power in the world should avoid;

- unofficial factual splitting of Ukraine according to the Transnistria, Ossetia or Abkhazia models, the government in Kiev ceasing to control large regions of its country – these being ruled by local pro Moscow regimes. Making allowance for the size of the regions and their economic and demographic importance, this means Ukraine losing its sovereignty both toward Brussels – in the western Ukraine – and toward Moscow – in the East and South Russian speaking regions. This strategy, in want of a compromise to save an independent Ukraine, is going on without an external intervention of Russia only by activating loyal local political forces shored up by the Russian military bases from Crimea.

Another major risk entailed by the Ukraine crisis consists in a possible deterioration of the Moscow – Berlin relation, one of the pivotal axes of a Eurasian project aiming to resurrect Europe. And besides the implications on Russia, an unstable situation in Ukraine plays into the hands of those attempting to prevent a rapprochement between Central Europe and Russia. All those wishing to maintain the present status of Germany as a military occupied country, more than 70 years after the end of the war, are keenly interested in hindering a closer cooperation between Central Europe and Russia, the sole possible ally having the military and political might needed to renegotiate the status of great power. And a Russia trying to come to after the communist nightmare is at the same time the natural ally of the traditional conservative European forces, possible one of the most feared enemies of the present system ruling the continent. Enforcing the strategy split and rule (from the Latin "divide et impera" a.n.) any fratricide conflict in Europe cannot but bolstering the present system and those behind it, United States and lately China.

At the same time, other three severe crises are rocking the world: ISIS, the migration to Europe of the civilians from the war zones in Asia, Middle East and North Africa, and the terrorist attacks aiming some of the European capital cities. Issues raising many questions both over the geopolitical future of the world and the role played by few secret services in this real doomsday scenarios.

This is in a nutshell the general geopolitical and geostrategic background of the present world the book "The Brotherhood of spies" comes out in. The more needed a book as long as the real universe of espionage is hard to get to and the literature in this field is deploringly scanty. A book openly supporting another universal truth all the denizens of this planet should know, namely that about all the espionage and counterespionage services all over the world confronting each other regardless whether belonging to allied or enemy countries.

The charge leveled against some information services over them "having spied on NATO," for instance, is not only preposterous but plainly laughable. All the services in the world had been are still are focuses on NATO and the former USSR. Nobody could and cannot make an exemption from this situation, in particular because in the world of espionage there are neither allies nor enemies. All are treated the same, being well known from the lessons history has taught us that "the allies of today could turn into the enemies of tomorrow," as happened after 1989.

In the current XXI century, all the states of the world should focus mainly on acquiring economic data, more than 95% of these being available from open, legal sources. Even if no more than 5%, acquiring secret data is of utmost importance. The espionage begins the very moment when acquiring highly valuable data entails breaking the law. The information services cannot forgo this if wishing to survive as state entity.

As to this side of the information services, namely of espionage, questions are not asked and answers are not being provided. The espionage services of a self-respecting country never sign any agreement to confine their total freedom of action. Israel, Japan, France, Germany, China and Russia undertake mainly economic spying activities on United States, the most natural thing in the world. United States and by and large the highly developed Euro-Atlantic space have plenty of data to pick up from.

If previously having referred to the North-Atlantic Pact, we stress that with or without the Washington agreement, as to the future of NATO there are certain signs about this organization not making it as "the main military security structure" in Europe. It looks like that by the development of the transatlantic relations in the last 25 years this assumption is gaining ground. Considering that in the last 67 years NATO has been the most brilliant jewel in the foreign policy crown of United States, that this military alliance has guaranteed the USA hegemony over Western Europe, in accordance to a concept of the people in charge at Washington about "those ruling Europe rule de world,"* the interest in maintaining and expanding this alliance is absolutely understandable. The military and political analysts on both shores of the Atlantic have grasped this being right the reason behind establishing NATO, and not de defense against "the communist expansion," as having been claimed during those 45 years of "cold war." If NATO would have limited itself to the role of a bulwark against the "communist danger," the alliance should have disbanded itself subsequently to the disappearance of the Warsaw Pact[23], the crumble of "the communist world" and the falling apart of former USSR, but this did not happen due to the staunch opposition of United States.

Under the sight of the whole world, the European Union is taking more and more shape as a superpower, mostly an economical one, as a centre of power of a new "multipolar world" in the making, bearing different visions and interests toward United States. Those still believing that both the expansion of NATO and the European Union are two complementing actions run the risk of being surprised and disappointed in the future.

An expanded NATO through the political will and exertions of Washington is to be a dysfunctional military alliance integrating the "Old Europe" represented mainly by France and Germany** United States can no more rely on, and "The New Europe" comprising former "enemy" states, members of the late Warsaw Pact, the Americans lay their hopes on to maintain their presence in Europe.

With the complex process of approving the European Constitution there is established a legal base to build on a European security system outside NATO. This is the main reason behind the Washington's frantic endeavors aiming to block the approval of the EU constitution through its influence agents from Poland, France and Holland. As a matter of fact, beginning with May 2006, the European Union Constitution Treaty gets ratified by Austria, Belgium, Cyprus, Estonia, Germany, Greece, Hungary, Italy, Latvia, Lithuania, Luxemburg, Malta, Slovakia, Slovenia and Spain.

The treaty forming the European Constitution had been signed by the representatives of the Member States on October 29, 2004, and was subjected to a ratification process in the Member States until 2005, when the French voters (May 29) and the Dutch ones (June 1) had rejected it in referendums.

The failing of the constitution project to gain popular support in the two aforementioned countries led to other countries defer or discontinue the ratification procedure, the future of the constitution looking bleak, to the satisfaction of the "White House" and its secret services. Had it been ratified, the treaty would have come into force on November 1, 2006.

Undoubtedly, as part of this dangerous game, the Eastward expansion of NATO and the European Union is an expression of this fierce underground struggle for spheres of influence on this side of the continent, struggle the Russian Federation takes part more or less conspicuously in. Logically thinking, we can say that an expanded European Union having its own constitution would not entrust its security into the hands of a non European power, even that being USA.

As long as it is still around, NATO will cease to be an alliance meant to defend the Euro-Atlantic zone against a foreign aggression, because such danger is no more present. Washington□s attempts to involve NATO in wars beyond its area of responsibility as defined by the Treaty of Washington from April 4, 1949, had failed and will stand no chances in the future, too. All NATO can do is to prevent wars breaking out among its own members. We can take into account a conflict between Spain and Great Britain over Gibraltar, but more probably one between Greece and Turkey, NATO□s "Achilles□ heel[24]." To this there can be added up the burden of potential conflicts among newly admitted member states, like the never ending dispute between Romania and Hungary over Transylvania.

Another basic truth overlooked by the political class of NATO☒s states is the North Atlantic Pact having never provided positive security guarantees to its members. This follows the article 5 of the Washington Treaty that had been negotiated one year with the Western Europe states, which turned down its initial wording but ended up accepting it under Washington☒s threats of denying them the benefactions of the famous Marshall Plan[25] if failing to accept it.

"The Parties agree that an armed attack against one or more of them in Europe or North America shall be considered an attack against them all and consequently they agree that, if such an armed attack occurs, each of them, in exercise of the right of individual or collective self-defense recognized by Article 51 of the Charter of the United Nations, will assist the Party or Parties so attacked by taking forthwith, individually and in concert with the other Parties, SUCH ACTION AS IT DEEMS NECESSARY, including the use of armed force, to restore and maintain the security of the North Atlantic area.

Any such armed attack and all measures taken as a result thereof shall immediately be reported to the Security Council. Such measures shall be terminated when Security Council has taken the measures necessary to restore and maintain international peace and security."

You are not supposed to be a law expert to realize that the expression SUCH ACTION AS IT DEEMS NECESSARY... removes any idea of "positive security guarantees" in this article. Such action deemed necessary by the signing party can be that of taking no measure at all.

For the first time in NATO's history the article 5 was called on over the horrific terrorist attacks against United States from September 11, 2001, but it produced no consequences.

As a general conclusion against this geostrategic background, "The Brotherhood of spies" shows us the way the spies and counter-spies has always been caught in the crossfire of the great battles waged in the past and present days for a NEW WORLD ORDER.

THE NEW WORLD ORDER

Whether or not controversial, in the democratic regimes the secret services are still a hotly debated issue. Their potential use as instruments – even in states ruled by law – by the political power leads to suspicions, in particular over the sincerity of the statements made on and on by their heads about their standing off politics. Here the controversy raised by the question: can or cannot be the secret services equated to the "political police" of a state? Worth mentioning is the fact that the already deeply entrenched expression "political police" made it to the list of political language employed by almost all belonging to the political class in the world. As a matter of fact, there is nowhere to be found a political police set apart from a repressive apparatus, for the plain reason that all the secret services in the world are faithful to the governments ruling them, being paid from the state budget. Accordingly, both CIA, and the Russian SVR, and the French DGSE and the Israeli Mossad, to name but some of the "heavyweights" of the world espionage, go into political police for the governments on which payroll they legally are.

Secondly, the "informative community" knack of eschewing, partially or entirely, the control exerted by the states ruled by law, as well as their penchant to go autonomous inside the structures of the same state stir suspicions on the legal nature of the various activities run by the secret services. That's why lately an American analyst was noticing the secret services in his own country "hiding, taking no responsibility over their actions while those in the government appointed to keep an eye on them hardly trust them."

Naturally, there⬚s no coincidence here. Against the background of tougher informative conflicts at the onset of this century and millennia the game played by the Great Powers on the world stage stands out more and more. A stage the New World Order steals the limelight on. Who, what and how is the New World Order? Where and when it turned up or was it talked about for the first time? These are the five pivotal questions seeking an answer in this book (too).

According to the modern theories, the New World Order is a global conspiracy led by political and financial power groups. The main idea underpinning the conspiracy theories over a new world order is that an occult global elite would aim to establish a world government to replace forthwith the sovereign national states governments and bring to an end the international struggle for power. On diverse significant political and financial events there had been spread rumors of having been planned by a very influent clique by way of many front organizations. Many historical and contemporary events are seen as stages of an ongoing plan to rule de world.

In the XX century, many chiefs of states and governments, topped by Woodrow Wilson[26] and Winston Churchill[27] had called on the term the "new world order" to refer to a new stage in the history of mankind bearing witness to a dramatic change in the political thinking of the world and shifting of the power balance after the First World War and the Second World War. They had seen these periods as an opportunity to enforce idealistic or liberal proposals for a global governance but in the sense of a new collective endeavors to identify, understand and work out the current issues beyond the possibilities of individual states. These proposals had led to the founding of several international organizations, among which is the "United Nations Organization"[28] and NATO, as well as the signing of some international agreements like the "Bretton Woods"[29] and the "General Agreement on Tariffs and Trades"[30] as initiatives aiming to maintain a balance between the world powers as well as for controlling the cooperation among nations, to usher a peaceful new era of capitalism. These initiatives and by and large the concepts of internationalism had always came under heavy criticism by the nationalistic, ultraconservative forces.

After the two world wars, the leftist political forces had hailed these newly established international organizations, but had affirmed they were marred by a deficit of democracy, being likewise not only inadequate to prevent the breaking out of a new world war but also unable to promote a global justice system. Accordingly, activists from all over the world had laid foundations of a federalist movement aiming to create a genuine new world order.

In 1940, the English science fiction writer Herbert George Wells[31] took a step further by appropriating and redefining the New World Order expression as synonym for establishing a scientifically administered global state ruled through a socialist type economic system.

In 1947-1957, time when the "Cold War" had reached new heights, theorists of the American secular and Christian right conspiracy had whipped up some ungrounded fears toward freemasons, Illuminati and Jews, these all being behind an international communist conspiracy.

The threat of a global communism in the shape of an atheistic state with a collective bureaucratic global government, demonized as the "Red Threat," turned into the main concern of the millennium apocalypse conspiracy supporters. Who are the players on this stage of the "New Order?"

THE APOCALYPSE CONSPIRACY AND MASONRY

For almost two millenniums, the Christian theologians and the laymen (persons not belonging to the clergy) have been afraid of a global conspiracy to lead to the fulfillment of the prophecies on the end of the world from the Holy Bible, in particular from the "Book of Ezekiel," the "Book of Daniel," the Jesus preach on the Olive Mountain, from the synoptic Gospels, as well as from the "Book of Revelation." They assert that human and demonic agents of the devil are involved into a primeval plot aiming to delude mankind over accepting a satanic theocracy to rule the world, the satanic theocracy of the "Unholy Trinity" – Satan, Antichrist and the lying prophet being the base of an imperial cult.

In many contemporary Christian conspiracy theories, the lying prophet would be the last pope of the Roman Catholic Church (enthroned by treason or through a Jesuit conspiracy), a charismatic guru from the "New Age" movement or even a leader of a Christian fundamentalist movement like "Fellowship"[32], while the Antichrist would be a president of the European Union, or the General Secretary the United Nations Organization or a virtual actor serving as front figure for a computer.

Freemasonry (or masonry), as institution, is an initiating order whose members are bound by commonly shared moral, spiritual and social ideals (in some cases even political ones), through initiation in accordance to a common ritual, through the oath taken on one of the holy books of the great religions ("Holy Bible," "Koran," "Dao de Jing"[33], "Hindus Vedas," "Buddhist Tripitaka" or other writings seen as sacred), and in most of the branches by the faith into a "supreme being", a "Great Architect of the Universe." The Masonic organizations in most of the country can be found as autonomous submissions, themselves consisting of blue lodges (knows as "workshops") of 7-50 persons (sometimes even more).

According to "The New Encyclopedia Britannica", freemasonry is the largest secret society (or "discreet society") in the world, spreading mainly in the XIX century along with the expansion of the British Empire.

The Illuminati Order (Illuminati) had been a secret society established on May 1, 1776 in Ingolstadt, Bavarian Kingdom, by the theology professor Adam Weishaupt. The movement had consisted of free-thinkers, liberals, republicans and feminists recruited from German Masonic lodges. In 1785, the order had been infiltrated, split and disbanded by the Bavarian authorities for a supposed plot aimed against all the monarchies and state religions from Europe. Weishaupt had been given political asylum at the court of a German prince.

"The Protocols of the Elders of Zion" (in original "Протоколы Сионских мудрецов") is a text put into circulation in the early XX century setting forth so called domination plans of the whole world devised by Jews. It had firstly been published in installments between August 28 and September 7 (old style) 1903 in the newspaper "Знамя" ("Znamia") from Sankt Petersburg. It is supposed that this theory was made up by the feared tsarist secret service Okhrana, upon the imperative order of the Tsar Nicholas II (his real name being Nikolai Alexandrovici Romanov, the last emperor of Russia).

The businessman Cecil Rhodes[34], promoter of the British Empire, had thrown his weight behind the idea of Great Britain re-annexing the United States with a view to establish a future imperial federation to rule de world militarily and politically. In his first will from 1877, written at the age of 23, he had expressed his wish to found a society (known as the "Electors Society") to further this aim.

In his 1928 book, "The Open Conspiracy," the British writer Herbert George Wells had called on the intellectuals from all over the world to come together to lay foundations of a future world federation aiming to strengthen democracy, awarding international citizenship, assuming an international authority between separate agencies at international level with a view to build a social-democratic world.

THE FOURTH REICH

"New Age" is a spiritual movement spread mainly in the Western countries, having his roots in the years 1920-1930 when Alice Bailey[35] had published several works proclaiming the return of Christ and introducing the necessary establishment of some groups which she was calling as of the global benevolence. Alice Bailey had foretold in 1940 the victory of the world war two Allies over the Axis Powers (victory taking place in 1945), as well as the founding by the Allies of a new world political and religious order. Bailey was seeing in the global federal government the culmination of Wells⊡ open conspiracy, but argued it being sinarchist since it would have been guided by the Great Masters of Ascension bent on preparing mankind for the second mystical coming of Christ at the dawn of Aquarius era.

According to Bailey, a group of masters called the "Great White Brotherhood"[36] is working on an inner esoteric plan to look over the passing to a new global order, but as of today the members of this spiritual hierarchy being known only by some initiates they would communicate telepathically with, but when necessary getting personally involved to let the whole world know about their presence on Earth.

In 1997, Rabi Yonathan Gershom, in an article titled "Anti-Semitic Stereotypes in the Writing of Alice Bailey," stresses that her aim (Alice Bailey's) is nothing but destroying Judaism. This is worth mentioning since the conspiracy theories are prone to depict the Jews as making up the main group wishing to establish the New World Order, plotters aiming more to repress than bring forth something beneficial.

The conspiracy theorists are also employing the expression "The Fourth Reich" as a derogatory synonym for the "New World Order" to imply that the state ideology and the world governance would be similar to the National-Socialist ones of the Third Reich. Furthermore, the Anti-Semites are using the expression to insinuate that a supposed future global government will be dominated by fascists and Jews.

Since the late 70⊡s, the extraterrestrials residing on other planets or coming from parallel dimensions (like the hypothetical beings from the "Gri race") and the intraterrestrials from the hollow centre of the Earth (like the "Reptilian race") had been included in the conspiracy theory on the "New World Order" and cast more or less consequential roles, as in the theories called down by the American authors Stan Deyo and Milton William Cooper and by the British author David Icke.

The promoters behind conspiracy theories speculate that the global elite in charge is made up of the modern upholders of Lucifer⊡s and follows a trans-human agenda aiming to develop and use human technologies to bring forth a post-human leading class; the speeding up to a new singularity technology would be so fast that the common people could not anticipate or make sense of the events occurring around them. The conspiracy theorists are afraid that the end result of this agenda would be the dawn of a New World – some sort of dystopia and/or the disappearance of mankind.

THE BELIEFS OF THE NEW WORLD ORDER

As there are several overlapping theories on the New World Order, there are around several beliefs about the way it would come to life. In general, the conspiracy theorists are those assuming the New World Order is carried out sequentially, and provide as examples in this sense the founding of the Central Bank of the United States ("the Federal Reserve") in 1913, the League of Nations in 1919, the International Monetary Fund in 1944, UN in 1945, World Bank in 1945, World Health Organization in 1948, the European Union – in the last two decades, the introduction of the Euro currency in 1993, the World Trade Organization in 1948 and the African Union in 2002.

The right American theorists of conspiracy, in particular those close to the United States radical militias, assume that the New World Order will be implemented through a dramatic coup d'état carried out by a secret team using black choppers, in the USA and other countries, to instate a totalitarian global government under UN control and imposed by foreign UN peace keeping forces. In accordance with the plans "Rex 84"[37] and "Operation Garden Plot"[38] this military coup would imply suspending the constitutions, imposing martial laws and appointing military commanders as chiefs of states.

The conspiracy theorists also believe that the New World Order is carried out by mass surveying programs, as well as through using personal numerical codes, products bar codes, universal merchandise marking codes, and lately through radio frequency identification techniques used in RFID[39] types microchip implants. After September 11, 2001 the American secret services have been recording daily 1.5 billion phone calls.

Skeptics warn about promoting consumerism, as for instance Katherine Albrecht and Liz McIntyre[40]. They assert that both governments and the great commercial companies plan to follow each movement of the consumers and RFID implemented citizens, which would amount to the last step taken to the totalitarian state surveying its own citizens like in the novel "1984" penned by George Orwell. That◻s why the Christians should stand against it since – as skeptics say – the databases and the modern communication technologies along with the commercial availability of sophisticated data acquiring equipments and authentication systems make possible today requiring related biometrical data or markings for acquisitions. They fear these modern technical possibilities look much alike the number of the beast foretold in the "Book of Revelation."

The conspiracy theorists on the right of Christians believe there is an occult old machination devised by the first Gnostics[41] and carried further by their successors, as the members of supposed esoteric circles: Cabalists[42], Cathars[43], the already famous Templar Knights[44], Rosicrucians[45], Freemasons, and not lastly the Illuminatis – who would attempt to undermine the Judeo Christian fundaments of the Western World to lay foundations of a New World Order through a "New Age" religion – a world readying the masses to embrace the new imperial cult of Antichrist. More at length, they assume that the globalists plotting in the name of a New World Order are using occult organization consisting of known superiors, spiritual hierarchies, demons, fallen angels or Lucifer. They believe that like the Nazi occultists, these conspirators are employing the power of the occult sciences (numerology), symbols (the Eye of Providence[46]), rituals (Masonic degrees), monuments ("National Mall"[47] marks), buildings ("Manitoba Legislative Building"[48]) and facilities ("Denver International Airport"[49]) to further their plot aiming world dominance.

Also, the conspiracy theorists believe that the New World Order will be enforced by controlling and surveying the persons[?] movements. That meaning that their plans aim to stem the development of societies through medical programs on health and family planning promoting abstinence, contraception and abortion, or cutting down purposely most of the world population via genocides triggered by futile wars, genetically engineered epidemic viruses and vaccines, as well as through ecological disasters entailed by changing meteorological conditions (example: HAARP[50]). "Codex alimentarius," a collection of world endorsed standards, practice codes, directions and other recommendations over edible products, food production and alimentary safety, turned likewise into an object of conspiracy theories about controlling population through starvation and diseases provoked by food introduced substances ("E numbers").

THE CULTURE OF FEAR AND THE GOD□S MONEY

The backers of conspiracy theory charge the governments, great companies and mass media of being part of a process intending to create an international consensus, and paradoxically, a culture of fear, since by an increased social control potential there would be instilled a fear among people towards this occult power. The greatest fear the conspiracy theory backers share is that of the conspirators using mind control – a wide range of techniques intended to deprive the individuals of their own thoughts, behaviors, emotions and decisions control – to carry out the new world order. These techniques would comprise everything, from the "Manchurian candidate," some kind of brain washing agent, up to psychological operations (fluoride water, subliminal publicity, Silent Sound Spreading Spectrum SSSS[51], MEDUSA[52]), as well as parapsychology operations (Stargate Project[53]) to influence the masses.

The idea of wearing a tinfoil hat as wave shield turned into a popular derided stereotype, being associated with conspiracy theorists. The skeptics hold that the conspiracy theorists fixation over population mind control, occultism, the great finance, the great occult, world government, is fostered by two factors, when a person:

1) bears strong individualist values, and

2) does not have this power.

The first attribute refers to those deeply concerned about a person's right to make his own decisions regarding his life without the interference of a higher system (for instance the state and its governments) and assuming no obligations imposed by the others. When the individualistic persons feel they cannot exercise their independence, namely being affected by a sense of helplessness, they undergo a crisis and grow overwhelmed by the thought that greater forces are responsible for having lost their independence.

In 2009, Pope Benedict XVI[54] said that behind the world financial collapse is the mindset of making profit regardless, and demanded the establishment of a New World Order for the "common good." In 2011 and 2012, based on this assertion, the Vatican made known it wishes a New World Order to be gradually implemented. The Vatican experts say a Global Central Bank is a must. Nothing new under the Sun!

Even since 1928 there is founded in Madrid "The Holy Cross and the Work of God" society (the famous "Opus Dei"[55]) which was taken over by the Pope and established links with Mafia. Inside the Catholic Church, according to several authors, the spiritual matters represent the mask it controls masonry, finance, trade, and therefore the world policy, under. It is worth noticing that "Banca di Santo Spirito"[56] is the oldest in the world, being founded by Pope Paul V in 1605[57].

Cultural critics, like Barkun[58], hold that the conspiracy theories have spread so fast due to many books, television serials and feature films, compounding suppositions and beliefs – theories defying general opinion – over the supposed establishment of a New World Order and bearing influence on the right extremists. Among these there are:

- Chris Carter, 1993-2008, "X Files" franchise, Richard Donner, „Conspiracy Theory," 1997 movie;

- Warren Spector and Harvey Smith (game designers): "Deus Ex," RPG from 2000;

- Dan Brown – "Angels and Demons," novel from 2000;

- Dan Brown – "The Lost Symbol," novel from 2009.

And now a natural question arises: what's the role played by the secret services in this insane struggle for power and world domination? To have a better grasp of the issue it must be said that by secret service, in accordance with the laws in force, there is understood a specialized state institution in the field of acquiring, checking and valorizing data needed for knowing, preventing and counteract any action posing a threat to a state's security. Their history is lost in the times of old, their existence paralleling the development of the armies and their need to have reliable information from the enemy territory. Among the first references about the usefulness of the secret services there can be reminded "The Art of War"[59] written by Sun Tzu[60]. This provides a detailed description of the role the spies are playing and the way they operate, as well as data on their recruitment.

"The spies are endowed, intelligent people, cautious and able to force their way to those who in the enemy camp are intimate with the sovereign and the nobility members. Thus they can notice the movements of the enemy and know his actions and plans. Once informed about the real situation they return to tell us."

(Sun Tzu – "The Art of War")

But let▯s not rush to conclusions…

THE "DAWN" OF ESPIONAGE

The roots of espionage cannot be dissociated from the world history it was a companion of both as to the pivotal events and the daily life happenings, so that many of the questions and answers of the past are closely intertwined with those of the present, and more likely than not of the future. That's why the universal history of espionage stirs not only the inquisitiveness of the present people but also their need to cast light on some of the puzzles and enigmas, mystifications and the myths they are facing, answering the necessity to foretell the dangers and errors threatening us.[I]

*

The first annotations on acquiring data seem to be those from the "Book of the Books," namely the "Holy Bible" which narrates some events related to what was later on known as espionage. Among other things is to be reminded chapter 13 from the "Fourth book of Moses," in the "Numbers" ("The Old Testament"), where it is shown that Moses had dispatched no less than 12 "agents," among which Caleb and Joshua, to the "Region of Canaan" encompassing then the actual territories of Israel and Jordan peopled with various tribes posing a potential danger to the Jewish people: "There[61] God said to Moses (13:3) < *Send thou men, that they may search the land of Canaan, which I give unto the children of Israel: of every tribe of their fathers shall ye send a man, every one a ruler among them.*>. 13:4" *And Moses by the commandment of the LORD sent them from the wilderness of Paran: all those men* were *heads of the children of Israel."* Therefore, the exertions made by the Jewish people to appropriate for themselves the "promised land", namely the entire territory the holy books were giving them, led to the necessity of sending spies to provide information on the military potential of the populations settling the land. First of all we refer to the Jericho[62] town on the bank of Jordan River [II].

According to the "Book of Joshua", the most important support the Jewish spies had benefited of in Jericho had been provided by a prostitute, Rahab, who looks like having been forced to take up this trade after being charged with sorcery. Rahab took upon herself hiding the Jewish spies from the local authorities. This promise had been stood by, the Israeli soldiers having to identify Rahab's house by a red ribbon at the window. It seems hence comes the red color the houses the prostitution, vying with the espionage for the title of the oldest trade in the world, had been practiced in were marked with.[III]

Still according to the "Holy Bible" there had been around women spies, too, working for foreign powers, traitors therefore, like Delilah, attending for the king of Philistines. Delilah had been commissioned to find out the secrets of Samson's strength, one of the "judges of the children of Israel". To ease her assignment Delilah became Samson's mistress, and after several attempts had learned the secret of his strength, lying inside his hair. While Samson was sleeping Delilah had cut off his hair so that the Philistines could lay their hands on him.

As a token of her treason for money, Delilah made it to art and literature, there being many paintings, musical compositions, literary works and movies the figure of one of the history's first women spies is immortalized in.[IV]

*

However, most of the espionage activities are going back to antiquity, the first sources on espionage coming from the ancient Egypt. The hieroglyphic annotations (on stone and papyrus) refers, inter alia, to acquiring information during commercial operations, to using agents for locating enemy populations to be conquered and enslaved.[V] And even more…

*

In the spring of 1274 BC, pharaoh Ramses II[63] of Egypt had learned the hard way what misleading and manipulation meant. It was in the fifth year of his reign[64] when the Hittite empire allied with Anatolia and Syria had decided to launch directly an attack against the northern territory of Egypt. The king of Hittites, Muwatallis II was in command of the allied forces consisting each of 18.000 foot soldiers and 2.500 chariots of war. Ramses was to strike back with an army of 20.000 foot soldiers and chariots of war. At a given moment two supposed deserters from the Hittite host had conveyed to the Egyptians false information over the enemy forces (revealing less than half of their actual strength), leading to the attack surprising the Egyptians utterly unprepared. And so a supposedly easy victory of the pharaoh turned into his finding himself along with the entire army encircled, hardly making it out from the trap set by the Hittites near the town of Kadesh (Syria).

From the first century AD the Egyptian espionage is focusing on the European rivals, Greece and Rome. Also in Egypt there are used for the first time message encoding systems, invisible inks or concealed pouch clothes. The Egyptian spies had called on plant extracted poisons and other substances for carrying out assassinates and sabotages.[VI]

*

The Greece Persian wars (V century BC) had their share of moments when the spying operations proved to be conclusive. Of great notoriety had remained the betrayal of Efialte, that who had guided the Persian host of 180.000 men of Xerxes I[65] over a hidden path going around the passing at Thermopile. Finding themselves surrounded on all hands the only option left to the 300 gallant Spartans[66] led by Leonidas[67] was the supreme sacrifice. And making thus history…

*

Alexander the Great[58], known also as Alexander Macedon (Alexander III of Macedonia or Alexandros III Philippou

Makedonon, king of Macedonia) was one of the greatest strategists and military leaders from history to find out the hard way the unquestionable value of espionage.

Lacking a well structured information service Alexander was close to lose the India campaign. Unknowing that the Indian army was using battle elephants he had a hard time conquering the resolution of his enemy. Learning from this potentially mistake, the Macedonian king had later on founded his own spy detachment. This had to inform on the enemy troops movements, their organization and equipment, on their tactics and readiness…

Furthermore, the spies of Alexander the Great had learned quite fast the trade of manipulation and misleading, as well as the way to find vital information not only on the enemy but on the morale in their own camp, too.

Thus, in 334 BC, when the Macedonian army was in full campaign against the Persian Empire, Alexander had learned about dissatisfactions among his soldiers. In an attempt to find the reasons behind them the Macedonian king had lifted the correspondence ban. After the couriers had left with the soldiers⬚ letters Alexander had them all detained and the entire correspondence given a thorough examination. That way there could be found not only the reasons that sparked the discontent but the names of those plotting against the king[VII], too. Later on, by doing away with the dissatisfactions marring the morale of his troops, Alexander the Great had carried out his campaign against Darius[69] up to its victorious conclusion.

*

In the work of Homer[70], the most intriguing narrations on espionage can be found in "Iliad"[71], in particular in "Chant X". There are depicted the dispatching of spies and some diversion and disinformation actions. To counteract the action of Palamedes[72], wishing the conclusion of the war, Ulysses[73] spreads the rumor of him having been bought by Priam[74], the king of Troy, making up a letter on behalf of that he wanted to compromise.[VIII]

A real diversion episode is undoubtedly that related to the "Trojan horse", operation prepared by sending an agent, Simon, to Troy, who tells the defenders of the fortress that the entrance of the "Trojan horse", an effective infernal machine, within the walls is aimed to quench the wrath of goddess Pallas Athens[75].

*

From ancient sources there comes out that the paternity of the information secret transmission system would belong to the Spartan leader Lysander, who is using an early form of secret writing on wax encased wooden tables to warn his citizens about a Persian invasion.[IX]

But no other ancient civilization had brought a more important contribution to the development of espionage than

Rome due to its having laid foundations of the greatest empire in Antiquity that could not be maintained and expanded without resorting to such means. From the first century BC there is mentioned the presence of a secret police, the so called "Frumentarii", also acting as censoring agency. There are employed "agentes in rebus" charged with counter-information operations. Worth noticing in this sense is the assessment of one of the researchers in the field of Antiquity, whereupon the Romans "*were highly skilled at political manipulations, espionage and dirty operations... Cover operations were something the Roman policy could not do without.*" [X]

Titus Livius[76] narrates about secret messages exchanges between Philip of Macedonia[77] and Hannibal[78] that had been intercepted by the Romans. He reminds us about Hannibal using to confuse the Romans by cooked up letters.

The bits of information acquired from deserters were checked by Hannibal with the assistance of his spies. Sometimes under guise, Hannibal was picking up and verifying information inside the enemy territory.[XI] It can thus be undoubtedly said that Hannibal had managed to organize and develop one of the most efficient information services in the ancient world.

The documents tell about the siege of a city in Syria, when Hannibal had sent inside a spy having the mission to light by night a fire in his hut and let thus the Carthaginian army know when to attack. And this operation is not by far unique, the army of Hannibal being preceded during the entire Italy campaign by hundreds of spies having to inform him on the Roman fortifications and fortresses, as well as about the defensive and offensive strength, the equipment and preparedness of the Roman army. But the famous Carthaginian general wanted even more... [XII]

As I previously wrote, Hannibal used to disguise himself, more often than not entering the enemy camp to apply later on some war tactics relative to the strength of his adversaries. The antique historians Polibius[79] and Titus Livius tell how the Carthaginians were tying lit torches to the horns of a bull herd to have the Romans take the movements of the herd for maneuvers of Hannibal's troops.

About the end of the second Punic war, the Roman army led by Scipio[80] landed in the North of Africa and attempted to conquer Cartagena for good. Subsequently to this campaign, Scipio became famous by taking over the harbor of Cartagena and through the victory against the army under the command of Hannibal in the battle of Zama[81]. Before that Scipio stood out by the many battles he had won in Spain. Intimate knower of military strategy, the Roman general owed his victories especially to a well set up spying system.

That's exactly what happened after the landing in the north of Africa, where Cartagena had had a strong ally in the person of Syphax[82]. Therefore, the Romans firstly had to defeat the Numidian army without Scipio knowing the manpower or the equipment of the adversary. Cunning, he had called on undercover informants, several centurions being disguised as slaves attending the general Gaius Laetius on a visit to the Numidia king (it is worth noticing that during the war Syphax had always vacillated between his status of ally and that of open enemy to Rome). As long as the two leaders had engaged in talks over signing a peace treaty the Roman spies had picked up pieces of information from the ground, these having the Roman commander reach the conclusion that a night attack could be the perfect choice. However, to get the necessary data, Romans had to improvise.

The Numidian king, of a very untrusting nature, had asked the Roman delegation not to leave the assigned accommodations and move through the camp but under the close surveillance of the Numidian soldiers. Seeing that the time goes by and the talks are drawing up to the conclusion, Laelius had ordered his scouts to stir up their own horses, so that the frightened beasts had tailed off from the Numidian camp. While "trying" to catch the horses the Roman "slaves" had enough time to learn thoroughly the fortifications of Syphax, the capital detail being that that the Numidians were building their huts using highly flammable materials (straws, reeds, wood). Coming under attack by night, with their camp set alight, the Numidians had been easily defeated by the seasoned Roman army.

Left without its strong Numidian ally Cartagena had to call back Hannibal from Italy, the only one still able to save the

North African state. Unfortunately, the Carthaginians had to wage the final battle in the terms set by Scipio, and so Hannibal went defeated for the first time, but decisively, at Zama.

Later on, by way of espionage too, there was found the place Hannibal was hiding in at Nicomedia and forced to commit suicide (186 BC).[XIII]

*

Another ancient episode, confirming the value of misleading and manipulation methods, had occurred in the III century when the Carthaginian host under the command of Hannon[83] found itself unexpectedly facing the uprising of 4.000 Gaelic mercenaries. These, disgruntled with not being paid on time had threatened to take the side of the Roman troops. Ruling out punishing the Gaels and triggering thus an open revolt, Hannon had applied a brilliant disinformation tactic. This had dispatched an "informer" to the Roman camp, who had "disclosed" the place the Carthaginians would supply fodder for their thousands cavalry horses in. At the same time, after working hard to calm them down, Hannon had sent the Gaels right to the place the Romans knew about from the "informer." Falling into the trap set by the Romans the Gaelic troops went wiped out; the issue the Carthaginian general had to face being worked out by his own enemies. Right against their would be allies in the fight to conquer Cartagena!

Another famous action brings to the fore the Roman general Ventidiu[84]. Being informed that a Parthian spy was in the Roman camp, the renowned Roman army commander spread a rumor about him fearing a Parthian attack from the field, where the roman legionnaires could hardly stand against the famous cavalry of the Parthian Empire[85]. Waiting for reinforcements, Ventidiu had to buy time to properly set up his lines of defense against the Parthian attack. Misled by the information coming from the Roman camp, the Parthians had preferred the field road (the longest) to the mountain one. This way Ventidiu had had enough time to get the troops dispatched to help him, the counteroffensive prepared by the Romans catching the Parthians off guard and leading in the end to their defeat.

*

Over several centuries a real cult of espionage grows in the ancient Rome, acquiring information being seen as a form of... art! A genuine "fashion" if making allowance for each Roman aristocrat having his own spies and trying to be always in the know as to the situation in the Senate. Later on, these authentic spy networks would be taken over and centrally organized, their only task being that of serving the interests of the Empire.

The first official secret service had been established from an officer corps commissioned to supply grain, the so called "frumentarii" I was writing previously about, during the tenure of emperor Domitian[86], or Hadrian[87], according to other sources.

Octavian Augustus[88], to be known later as Octavian(us), the first self proclaimed Emperor of Rome, had seen the informative networks as of utmost importance. Though preserving the state form of the Roman Republic, successfully patronizing his large informative networks, Octavian(us) led like a dictator for more than 40 years. Well informed, he knew what decisions to take in order to bring to and an end a century of civil wars and usher in a much awaited for era of peace, prosperity and imperial grandeur. He is known by the historians under the title Augustus, which he entrusted upon himself in 27 BC, at the same time being seen as the "father" of the Roman postal service, establishing in century I BC a parcel and postal service named "cursus publicus".

Through this movement the information conveying system got streamlined and the emperor?s security and state?s stability had been provided. During the following decades the Roman emperors had been entrusting delivery attributions and foreign espionage duties to some members of their personal guard called "speculatores" (observers). Through the power they came by these had turned in time into a real "political police," their missions ranging from wiping out and assassinating political adversaries to persecuting the Christians. Moreover, by collaborating with the other coercive forces they had been granted the right to perform arrests all over the Empire provinces.

Diocletian[89], becoming aware of the serious abuses the "frumentarii" had been responsible for had ordered a large reshaping of the informative structures by replacing these with the so called "agentes rebus", public functionary civilians. The new service was demilitarized and enjoyed a greater autonomy than the previous one.

In conclusion, by following the development of data acquiring in the Ancient Egypt, Babylon, Numidia, Cartagena, the Persian, Parthian and Phoenician empires, the Romans had taken over from other civilizations they came in contact with and improved these techniques to gain an informational edge. But their misuse led to effects antagonistic to those envisaged, so that, ironically, despite their sound repute as builders and engineers the Romans had never been as good in keeping an eye open on their enemies as those had been in their reciprocal spying.

*

But the Romans had been not the only ones to stand out in the espionage techniques. One of the most famous leaders of antiquity, Mithridates[90], had always relied upon an exquisitely set up information service. Ascending to the throne of his parent at an early age, this is ousted and forced into exile[XIV]. After having been travelling the Asia Minor countries for several years, where he taught himself diligently (he was fluent in 22 languages and dialects of that time), Mithridates regains his throne and wreak a terrible revenge right on his mother and her relatives.

To avoid in the future being again caught off guard by the machinations in the Palace, Mithridates had laid foundations of a real secret service. Fierce adversary of Rome, skilful leader and shrewd manipulator, the king (despot) of Pont knew to win the hearts and minds of the many people conquered by the Roman troops.

His secret agents were acting day in day out both in the Asian provinces of the Roman Empire and the Greek territory, so that Mithridates had only to win from the relentless exploitation and the disaffections of the people in the aforementioned regions.

But the greatest advantages he obtained from the pieces of information provided by his spies from the "Eternal City." In the thick of a civil war waged between Marius[91] and Sylla[92] parties, Rome was the stage of never ending disorders. Knowing beforehand what events were to take place, Mithridates had exploited to his own benefit the weaknesses of the Romans and expanded thus his empire. Nevertheless, the face-off between Mithridates❒ and Romans❒ spies was won by the latter, situation that led, after three bloody wars, to the final defeat of king Mithridates, the losing of his possessions, and not lastly, to his suicide.

One of the vanquishers of Mithridates, and I named Sylla, had been in his turn known for the importance he gave to espionage. Not only a seasoned general but also an influential political character, Sylla had realized he was in no position to defeat his enemies without large spy networks, acquiring data being pivotal during those troubled days of the Roman Empire. Having informers among the slaves of the Roman aristocracy he was representing as leader of the Optimates Party, among those of his eternal rival Marius, but also among the soldiers and courtiers of Mithridates, Sylla had succeeded in foiling several attempts at his life and gain important victories on the battlefields of Antiquity.

*

Caius Julius Caesar[93] made history as one of the promoters of espionage. Before starting off a military campaign Caesar was seeking detailed information about the country he was to conduct military operations in. He was interested in the customs, political institutions, history as well as the economy of the country. To this end, Caesar himself mentions several times in the seven volumes of his work "De Bello Gallico" the usefulness of using secret agents, in particular merchants. In the time of Caesar, the necessity of informative activities had also its correspondence in the setting up of his legions. Each of them were comprising 10 spies or scouts bringing up the rear of the cavalry charges to pick up information about the territory and the population most of the Roman army had to fight against.

Diverse informative methods had been used by Caesar during his confrontations with internal enemies, as a matter of fact his former allies, in the civil war. For instance, we refer to the battles waged against Pompeius[94]. In the enemy camp there had been dispatched spies having to inform on the financial means at their disposal. It looks like Caesar had had the greatest number of spies and informers known up until then.

However, Julius Caesar had failed to always use properly the information available, situation that in the end proved to be his undoing. On the day of his assassination Julius Caesar had been informed by a spy about the plot against him, but he waved it away and was killed.

The Roman leader had had an encoding system, too, known as "Caesar's alphabet," based on letter substitution. Plutarch[95] (in his work Parallel Lives) shows that Julius Caesar was one of the first to use the cipher.[XV]

*

Information acquiring actions had been performed in the time of the Dacians, during the reign of king Decebal[96]. According to some accounts this had sent from Dacia[97] to Rome one of his agents who managed to get elected to the Roman Senate[XVI]. This happened due to the gold he had lavishly given to the Roman politicians of that time. It cannot be ruled out that the first Dacian-Roman war (101-102 AD) came to an inconclusive end in consequence of the actions undertaken by this agent of Decebal's, named Atticus.

Dio Cassius[98] narrates some espionage episodes during the wars against Dacians. After the first of them, Domitian (Titus Flavius Domitianus), Roman emperor of the Flavian family (81 - 96 BC), receives a letter on behalf of Decebal whereby he admits his defeat. Domitian shows this letter to the Senate to prove his victory. But in fact the letter had been forged by Domitian himself to stress his achievements. But there is also possible the letter having been sent by Decebal for misleading purposes.

On Decebal, Dio Cassius said: "*He was skilful at war planning and adroit in carrying them out, sage in picking out the opportunity to attack the enemy and fall back on high time. He was cunning in setting traps, gallant in battle, knowing how to take wisely advantage of victory and pull unscathed through a defeat. Out of this reason for a long time he was a feared enemy of the Romans.*"

The same author depicts the way Decebal managed to block through the Roman legions advancing to Sarmizegetusa Regia (the capital city of the Dacian Kingdom): "*Decebal feared the victorious Romans marching toward his capital. That's why he felled the trees around to a given height and laid weapons on the trunks for the enemies to think there were soldiers and beat a hasty retreat. And that indeed happened,*" says Dio Cassius.

*

As I previously wrote, we cannot conclude the review of the main informative confrontations of antiquity without reminding that the first espionage treatise belongs to Sun Tzu. This had lived about 25 centuries ago and stood out as author of an exquisite work on the "art of war" titled "The Thirteen Commandments." The book proves the high level the strategy and tactics of the informative activities had achieved in the ancient China.

The thoughts of Sun Tzu about the "art of war" and espionage stem from pragmatic ideas: *"What we call caution cannot be obtain either from gods or spirits, or through analogy with past events or reckonings, but through the assistance of people knowing the enemy position."* Accordingly, one of the most important issues Sun Tzu was concerned with related to the qualities an agent must possess[XVII]. This fell into one of the 5 categories of secret agents that could be used in a face-off, namely: indigenous, interior, double, dispensable (sacrificial) and mobile.

Sun Tzu thought that *only an enlightened sovereign and an appreciated general able to use as agents the most brilliant persons could achieve great results,* claiming that *the secret operations are essential in war, the army relying on them to perform its maneuvers.*

Contemporary with Sun Tzu, the Chinese general Chia Lin stated that an army *without secret agents is like a man without eyes and ears.*

THEODORA, COMMANDER IN CHIEF OF THE BYZANTIUM ESPIONAGE

Turned from dancer and courtesan into empress of Byzantium by marrying the emperor Justinian[99], Theodora[100] bears an important political influence on her husband. She sets up in particular a network of informers inside and outside the empire. When in 532 an uprising ("Nika"[101]) breaks out in Constantinople (today Istanbul), the capital of the empire, by means of her spies Theodora availed herself of information to negotiate and ward off the danger, saving thus the throne of Justinian.

It is told that Theodora was personally assisting to the training of her spies, forcing upon them an oath of unconditional faith: *"If failing to carry out my orders you will be skinned alive."* The information service founded (in Byzantium[102]) by Theodora carried on its activity throughout the following centuries, bearing some influence on the future setting up of this kind of agencies.[XVIII]

CASSOCK SPIES

Since its inception, the Catholic Church came to be a force to be reckoned with in the field of espionage. Possessing a large and efficient bureaucratic apparatus and important resources, it could overlook some informative operations, establishing a real spy network. The prevalence of church in the field of espionage had been challenged during Renaissance[103], when the strengthening of the centralized states stood behind them taking the initiative and laying the foundations of their monopoly and dominance in this field with a view to protect their own political, military, but also economical and commercial interests[XIX]. A telling example would be that of the great medieval powers.

GENTLEMAN SPY

The onset of the English espionage/counterespionage, and to a large extent of the European ones, dates back to the Middle Age, when during the tenure of Henry VII[104], the ambassadors or the special envoys of London had had also responsibilities related to acquiring information. Likewise, in that time we can talk about professional spies, as well as of structures and informative agencies headed by Cardinal Thomas Wolsey[105] and Thomas Cromwell[106].

Characteristic to the English espionage of that time was the important representatives of cultural life getting involved in informative activities. Thus, one of the best known Renaissance spies was Pierre Alamire (1470 - 1536), composer, engineer, diplomat and spy on the payroll of Henry VIII[107]. It is probably less known that the poet and playwright Christopher Marlowe[108] was an agent at the service of Queen Elisabeth I[109], what is called a "gentleman spy."

The England ambassador to Paris, sir Edward Stafford[110], had been seen as one of the first double diplomatic agents. The greatest achievement of Prior Matthew (1664 - 1721), priest and diplomat, was setting up a spy network in France. Taking into account the naval power of the "Albion," from this lineup of agents there could not be missing a sailor, John Deane (1679 - 1762), spying in Russia.[XX]

THE MASTERS OF THE ELIZABETHAN ESPIONAGE

Returning to the secret world of the time of the England⊠s Elisabeth I, many can be said about her, the most important thing being her making history. Dominated by the personality of Lord Francis Walsingham[111], the man in charge of the kingdom⊠s secret services, an internationally renowned spy and the royal lover bedding the sovereign longest, this world led to the occurring and later consolidation of the greatest global power of that epoch: the British Empire!

In order to bolster the monarchic power and state influence both internally and externally, the Elizabethan secret services had managed, by employing many undercover agents, to come in possession of valuable pieces of information shedding light on the close ties between the court of the French king and the Catholic forces from England and Scotland in particular. After the Pope in Rome had "excommunicated" Elisabeth I, an unparalleled recrudescence of the conspiratorial actions inspired and supported at the court of the French king by the Jesuits, aiming inter alia to physically eliminate the "heretic queen" from London, had been recorded.

The information provided by the English spy network led to thwarting some assassination attempts on the queen, as well as to the wiping out of the internal catholic movements aiming to put Mary Stuart[112], an earnest catholic and queen of Scotland, on the throne of England. Furthermore, by the counter-informative endeavors of its secret services, England had kept at bay the civil war that had threatened it years on end.

But the exploits of the English spies and counter-spies go beyond that. Through agents implanted at the court of the Spanish king Philip II[113] the secret services learned that the England ambassador in Paris, Sir Edward Stafford, was spy at the service of Spain. This had been recruited by the espionage service of the Spanish Monarchy shortly after his arrival to the French capital, in exchange of a hefty sum of money.

The English espionage had reacted by placing near Stafford of a well trained agent of its named "Roger", who had "intoxicated" Sir Edward Stafford with information specially concocted for the King of Spain by the English counterespionage. In present terms it comes that the betraying ambassador had been turned unknowingly into an intoxicating agent of King Philip II of Spain and the Spanish espionage service. In a nutshell, a "useful idiot!" This way, by providing the Spaniards no reasons to get suspicious and avoiding undermining the political prestige of England, Sir Stafford had been gratified for services he made unawarely to England by having never been brought to trial for treason and let to grow old undisturbed and with his repute unblemished.

Another great achievement of the Elizabethan espionage was gaining information proving that the Catholic Party in France under the authority of Duke de Guise[114] had masterminded an escape plan of Mary I Stuart from her detention place, she being also a nephew of the French leader. In order to acquire pieces of information as detailed as possible over this plan, and in particular the names of the conspirators in England collaborating with the Catholic circles from the continent, the English secret services had dispatched to Hexagon one of their most brilliant agents, the playwright Christopher Marlowe, of whom I was writing in the preceding chapter, friend and colleague of William Shakespeare[115].

Marlowe left for his mission as a "Cambridge student" with strong "Catholic convictions," therefore an open "enemy" of Queen Elisabeth I. He "ran away" from England for being "persecuted" and wishing to resume his studies in Reims, France, where had been established the most influential Jesuit Catholic centre and the plan to "liberate" and bring to Paris Mary I Stuart had also been devised.

The story told by Christopher Marlowe proved credible, the English agent being let to join the movement. After having remained enough time at the Jesuit Seminary in Reims to get the necessary information, being admitted in the ranks of the plotters, Marlowe had returned to England. Throughout his mission to France the playwright Christopher Marlowe had played the role of a penetration agent, role only the brilliant spies can play.

On the strength of data brought from France by Christopher Marlowe and some material evidences (letters of Mary I Stuart to her catholic supporters from France and Spain) fetched by the English secret service agents through intercepting the diplomatic correspondence of the France and Spain ambassadors to London, charges serious enough to led to the beheading of Mary I Stuart had been issued. And along with the head of Mary I, the Queen of Scots, the heads of many English noblemen had also fallen, to the fore being that of Lord Babington[116], the most important of those that had attempted to the life of Queen Elisabeth I.

As expected, the French espionage and the Jesuit circles did not forgive Christopher Marlowe, and in May 1593, in a pub from Deptford, somewhat close by Greenwich, on the bank of Thames, at the age of only 29, the talented playwright had been assassinated.

For laymen, Christopher Marlowe, high class spy of the Elizabethan time, had been the most important precursor of William Shakespeare, having penned some famous plays like "Tamburlaine" (1588), "The Jew of Malta" (1590) and "Doctor Faustus" (1592). It is assumed that Christopher Marlowe had closely cooperated with William Shakespeare on writing some of his plays, among which "Titus Andronicus" and "Henry VI".

The English spies of that time had succeeded, under diplomatic cover, as merchants or "religious political opponents" of the protestant queen Elisabeth I, in not only penetrating the courts of the king of France and Spain, but also the Jesuit Order centers and the intimate circle of the Pope.

Furthermore, in the name of the English Crown they had established sound political and diplomatic relations with the tsarist Moscow and took up an intense trade with the inner Russia through the "English Muscovy Company"[117]. Also, the English spies had gained the benevolence and support for England from the powerful sultans at Istanbul and made it up to the Mogul monarch courts in India.

The Elizabethan espionage had established a very efficient surveying system of the sailing routes from Atlantic and around the Cape of Good Hope (southern tip of Africa), of the naval bases in Spain, and in particular that of Cadiz, as well as of the Spanish colonies from the "New World"[118]. On the strength of the gained information the English fleet had been setting up years on end under the command of freebooter-admiral Francis Drake[119] lighting piracy style attacks on the Spanish galleons sailing back to the country brimming with priceless loads of gold, silver and precious stones.

Despite its many successes, by far the "pearl" of the Elizabethan espionage crown was that of acquiring detailed information on the invasion planned by Philip II and the Catholic Church against England, data that led to the glorious English victory in the face of the "Invincible

Armada"[120] and calling off the landing of the Spanish troops under the command of the Duke of Parma[121].

For those liking this genre, I recommend the series "Spies of the <Virgin Queen>" (8 volumes) relating to the historical background and the restive, mysterious and exciting world of the spies and the freebooters in the Elizabethan time. According to the author, in those volumes we will find both information and real characters from the medieval epoch of Queen Elisabeth I and fiction.

RICHELIEU□S AGENTS

Like England, France, that was also undergoing a process of strengthening internally the centralized power while externally attempting to counteract the influence and possible hegemonic tendencies of other Great Powers (in particular England□s), had endeavored to establish and organize espionage operations. Peculiar to France was the involvement both of the church leaders and the state in such actions. The most important spy of Richelieu□s[122] was Pater Joseph, influence agent on behalf of France. Some of Richelieu□s agents had been source of inspiration for the characters in the novels penned by Dumas-father[123], like countess of Carlyle, an agent in France Milady de Winter had been drawn from. But the successor of Richelieu, Cardinal Jules Mazarin[124], had had his spies, too, like Melani, influence agent at the court of Ferdinand of Bavaria[125].

There had been instances, some less known, when French diplomats had worked closely with religious and cultural personalities of that time. It is the case of the France ambassador to London, who at a given time is being paid a visit by the Italian priest Giordano Bruno[126], that who would end up on the pyre in consequence of the heretical convictions he was entertaining. That had arrived to London in 1583 on a secret mission, as it comes out from his traveling under a "codename" (Henry Fagot) and wearing a mask.[XXI]

THE SECRET... PAINTER!

Another Great Power of that time, Spain, had to get involved in the "secret war" of the spies. Bernardino de Mendoza (1540 - 1604), a sophisticated personality of that time, officer, military historian, diplomat, had acted in England, while Willem von Ripperda (1680 - 1738) in Holland. Likewise, there is less known that the great painter Peter Paul Rubens[127] had activated as a secret messenger, too.[XXII]

The informative approaches of Vienna in that time had been related to the two sieges of the Austrian capital (by the Turks). Georg Franz Kolschitzky (1640 - 1694), a Polish nobleman (his real name - Jerzy Franciszek Kulczycki), who had gained important pieces of information from the Ottoman camp he was skulking unnoticed into during the 1683 siege of Vienna, had made history. As reward he was allowed to open the first coffee shop in Vienna.

THE WALLACHIAN SPIES

In this medieval world of machinations and intelligence gathering endeavors, few know the important role played by the Romanian Provinces[128], in consequence of their geostrategic position these having been engaged in or subjected to espionage actions. Intelligence gathering abroad had been warily resorted to by the Romanian princes Basarab I[129], Mircea the Elder[130], Vlad the Impaler[131], Stephen the Great[132], Vasile Lupu[133], Serban Cantacuzino[134] and Constantin Brancoveanu[135] not to call forth the reaction of the Ottoman Empire[136] or of other contiguous Great Powers.

On the Kahlenberg rise close by Vienna there had been set an inscription bearing the following text: *To the memory of the Romanian soldiers who in the year 1683, during the siege of Vienna, had their share of contribution to the relief of the city.* Nurturing the hope to shake off the High Porte sovereignty but unable to get plainly involved in the battles, the Prince of Wallachia (historic province of Romania), Serban Cantacuzino (1678 – 1688), and that of Moldavia (another historic province of Romania), Gheorghe Duca[137], picked out the path of informative approaches, espionage and even sabotage (replacing the guns⬚ shots with straws), acting as "double agents", to use a modern terminology. Thus, Serban Cantacuzino had mediated both the movement of the Imperial couriers and that of the information, letting the Austrians know in due time that the Turks had run short of the resources needed to carry on the siege.

Stolnic[138] Constantin Cantacuzino (1655 – 1716) had been one of the scholars of that time who had taken up informative actions, becoming the man in charge of what could be seen as the first service of this kind in the Romanian Principalities, the present day Romania. Among the activities taking place at the Secret Chancery he had set up at the Old Court[139] there could be included: receiving agents bringing information from other countries, editing, translating and "opening" the secret correspondence. As a matter of fact, the Stolnic had also made up a "cipher". The Palace at Mogosoaia[140] (near Bucharest – the capital city of Romania) was more often than not hosting secret meetings with foreign envoys, sometimes under guise, later on being directed to leave on secret paths. An exquisite skill of the Great Steward was that of worming out information from foreign interlocutors without them realizing that, in particular during feasts wine was lavishly provided to the guests. [XXIII]

*

Another outstanding intellectual involved in informative activities, probably the first Romanian to have activated in different countries, was Nicolae Milescu Spatarul[141]. Grigore I Ghica[142] had appointed him as diplomatic agent (capuchehaie) at the High Ottoman Porte. Milescu had acted as influence agent for the former prince Gheorghe Stefan[143]. He got used to the ways of "the diplomatic espionage" at manifold European courts. These had been probably the reasons why upon the recommendation of Dosithei, the Patriarch of Jerusalem, Milescu had been admitted among the courtiers of the Tzar of Russian, Aleksei Mihailovici[144], who would dispatch him on a secret mission to China to pick up information and establish confidential political relations or, as specified in the mandate (imperial ukase) handed to him, *to undertake researches, employing any suitable means, among all those in the know and find out the genuine truth.* (...)[XXIV]

One of the most mysterious personalities of the European espionage had once ascended the throne of Moldavia. Gaspar Graziani[145] had been a faithful attendant of the Ottoman Porte which entitled him dragoman[146] and sent him on a mission to the Habsburg Empire[147]. These merits, mostly of an informative nature, had the Sultan appoint him to the throne of Moldavia after having gone from Catholicism to Orthodoxy. But nevertheless Graziani betrays the High Porte by beginning talks with the king of Poland Sigismund III Vasa[148], having thus the Ottoman Empire removing him from the throne.

*

The fact that the Romanian Principalities had been of interest for the European powers is proven by the presence here of some agents. Among others we talk about Matteo Murano (? – 1503), physician, but in fact agent for Venice, who had arrived in August 1502 at the court of Stephen the Great to provide medical treatment for the prince of Moldavia. Some medieval sources make clear reference to the Moldavian great prince having been assassinated by Murano through the use of a poisoned "miraculous" ointment. The order would have been issued straight from the highest hierarchy of the Catholic Church after the assurances given by the Great Stefan to the Ottoman Porte about him not interfering anymore in a future conflict between Christians and Turks. Reason why "the Champion of Christendom"[149] of yesteryear turns public enemy number one for Vatican. (…)

*

Especially in the late XVII century the expansionist plans of the Habsburg Empire regarding the Romanian Principalities led to the presence here of some Vienna agents, like the abbot Giovanni Baptista del Monte in Wallachia at the court of Serban Cantacuzino (1678 – 1688), on a mission to influence the Romanian voivode into concluding an Anti-Ottoman agreement with Austria, or Bartolomeo Ferrati, physician at the court of Constantin Brancoveanu but in fact heading a network of informers in Buchares[150] and Iasi[151] to the benefit of the Court in Vienna.

The espionage, informative activity of the Habsburg Empire in the Romanian Principalities heightens and grows better organized along with the establishment in 1782 of the diplomatic agencies. Austrian consuls and those of other Great Powers were conveying valuable data, mostly regarding the intentions of the Ottoman Empire, acquired by way of the informer networks from the Romanian

Principalities. For instance, in March 1794, "the commercial" agent Markelius writes to the Austrian chancellor, Kaunitz[152], over "the money needed to pay our agents."

But in the Romanian Principalities there were acting agents of Prussia and England, too, these coming thus to be an important place on "the secret war" map, and remaining so during the following centuries.[XXV]

THE ESPIONAGE OF THE EMPIRES

The so called "time of the empires" between 1700 and 1900 brought along the naissance of the modern espionage, embodied by setting up services, efficient intelligence agencies, and distinguished through the activity of some professional agents who had left their mark on several historical events. In the XIX century the secret services of Great Britain came of age and grew adapted to the needs of the Albion. In 1844 there is established the "British Intelligence Service" while in the second half of the century distinctive agencies in the field of data acquiring and counter-information sprang up, too.

England had probably been the Great Power that succeeded in undertaking espionage actions throughout Europe and beyond since XVII century by means of agents who can be seen as real personalities both in this field and the cultural one. For instance, we refer to Aphra Behn (1640 – 1689), also called the "Incomparable one", one of the first professional women writers from English literature and at the same time spy at the service of England, in particular in the Low Countries. Another cultural personality engaged in informative actions had been the father of Robinson Crusoe, Daniel Defoe[153], seen as one of the founders of the British intelligence service.[XXVI]

Of the Napoleonic wars spies, France having obviously been the target, worth reminding here are the diplomat William

Wickham (1761 – 1840) and Count d⬚Antreg, who had been a double agent, too.

THE EXPLORERS "007"

An important role in undertaking informative actions, even beyond Europe, had been played by the explorers, among them both scientific personalities of that time and masters of espionage, trail blazers for the British colonial expansion.

Of the more famous examples worth reminding here are those of William Moorcroft (1767 – 1825) regarded as a pioneer in mapping Himalaya, and Francis Younghusband (1863 – 1912), who had played an important role in the exploration of the roads to India and China. Deemed as one of the most capable spies England had had in the XIX century, Francis Richard Burton (1821 – 1890) was at the same time both an exquisite explorer and man of science in Middle East and Africa, having also translated the fairy tales collection from "One Thousand and One Nights."[XXVII]

THE SPY QUEEN

In the time of regality, revolution and Napoleonic wars France stood out, in accordance with its interests and ambitions, as one of the Great Powers on "the secret front" too. Such active attitude went on unswervingly during both the Empire and the Republic. Of all the modern secret services, the French "Deuxième Bureau"[154] established in 1874 was the one to get close to the achievements of the British Intelligence Service[155]. However, there had been failures and corruption cases that cast a shadow on its activity, for instance the "Dreyfus Affair"[156].

Louise de Keroualle (1649 – 1734), deemed as "the best known of the French woman spies" in the XVII century, stood out since youth not only through her beauty but also through her uncommon intelligence which afforded her becoming the sweetheart of Frederick, the Prince of Wales[157], but also an agent by him. XXVIII

Of course, the activity of the "the disguised spy" Charles Éon de Beaumont (1728 – 1810), agent of the royal secret service (Secret du roi) in Russia and England, cannot be overlooked either.

PEN... SPIES!

Cashing in on their prestigious literary activity, some writers of that time went mostly into action as "influence agents." This is the case of François-Marie Arouet (known as Voltaire[158]) who had played such role by Frederic II[159], the King of Prussia, or the father's of "Figaro", Pierre Augustin Caron de Beaumarchais[160], agent of King Louis XV[161] in England. [XXIX]

The "great lover" and author of memoirs Giovanni Giacomo Casanova[162] had also been engaged in espionage activities against England. The abbot and writer François Xavier Montesquieu[163], member of the French Academy, came to be the main agent of the future king Louis XVIII[164].

THE BETRAYAL OF NAPOLEON

Besides his regular army, the consul and the future emperor Napoleon[165], had maintained also an army of spies, among whom was Ludwig Schulmeister (1770 – 1853). Despite his successful actions against Austria Napoleon had denied him The Legion of Honor: *I can give you money but I can?t decorate a spy.*

But some of his spies had betrayed the emperor, as for instance "the prince of the diplomats", Charles Maurice de Talleyrand-Perigord[166], who despite being for long in charge of the French foreign policy went also into spying activities for Russia and Austria.

Accordingly, among "the diseases" the intelligence services would go through up until now is "duplicity," "the double game." Probably the heads of the French counterespionage would have carried on accusing Dreyfus of espionage for Germany to cover thus the real spy, Ferdinand Walsin-Esterhazy, if few personalities, genuine patriots like writer Emile Zola[167], had not gone engaged in laying open those machinations.[xxx]

THE ARMY OF 10.000 SPIES

Along with the policy of uniting Germany and gaining a proper international status for it, chancellor Otto von Bismarck[168] went interested in establishing an intelligence service that ended up with about 10.000 agents in its ranks dispatched to many European countries! Among them was that who could be seen as a predecessor of industrial espionage, Johann Gotfried Brügemann (1750 – 1802), who had stolen the secret of the loom from England, but also baroness Kaulla (1850 – 1910), who became mistress of the France Minister of Defense.

*

One of the most important personalities of "the secret front" had certainly been the Austrian chancellor Klemens von Metternich-Winnerburg (1773 – 1859), who at least for awhile could be considered as "the master spy" of the European continent. He missed not the chance to prove his skills at the Vienna Congress, aiming to establish the new organization of Europe after the Napoleonic wars. On this occasion several of the participants, among whom there were important politicians and diplomats from all over Europe, offered themselves to provide information to the Austrian chancellor.

Another great spy of that time was considered the officer Alfred Redl (1864 – 1913) one of the most efficient planted agents ("mole") who had spied for Russia over 12 years. As a matter of fact, recent investigations have "debunked" to a large extent this myth, Redl being remembered both as a precursor of a homosexually prone category of agents and also as the spy that had done an inexcusable series of errors which in fact led to his "falling"[XXXI] However, Redl is still talked about as the man that had furthered the introduction of new global data acquiring methods, fact that led to his appointment, at the peak of his career, as head of the Vienna Secret Service he was in charge of between 1907 – 1912.

BENJAMIN FRANKLIN HAD SPIED FOR ENGLAND!

On the other shore of the Atlantic, the rising of the United States of America began against the background of informative undertakings, the first major events having been triggered by spies. On "the invisible front" of that war important agents stood out. Hence, England had "cashed in on" the services of some active spies like Benedict Arnold[169], who despite being close to George Washington[170] had chosen to spy for the English in return of a large sum of money.

Surprisingly, even one of the "founding fathers of the country", well known diplomat, man of science, inventor, philosopher and politician, Benjamin Franklin[171] had been at least for a while, in particular when ambassador to London, agent for England, which he sent important pieces of information.[XXXII]

But the American states had also activated on this "front" with capable agents, as it was Robert Townsend (1754 – 1838) who had provided important pieces of information to the American troops, or Lydia Darragh (1753 – 1789), who by passing on intelligence coming right from the English General Staff had bolstered the position of the military units under the command of George Washington.

"LA BELLE REBELLE" AND "THE WILD ROSE"

It can be said this civil war had paved the way for a substantial engagement of the women agents in informative activities. Hence, most of the agents on the Union side (the northern states) had been women: Pauline Cushman (1833 – 1893), interred with military honors for the services provided, Mary Elizabeth Bowser (1839-?), seen as "one of the most efficient spies", or Harriet Tubman, probably the first African American spy, born in bondage, in the history of the United States.[XXXIII]

But many women agents had also activated for Confederation (the southern states), among whom are actress Belle Lloyd ("La Belle Rebelle"/1844 – 1900), the spy that had conveyed a large amount of information, or the beautiful widow Rose Greenhow ("The Wild Rose" /1817 – 1874), the most important figure of the South spy network.

RIGGED ELECTIONS

Standing against the unification of the Romanian Principalities[172], the Moldova caimacam[173] Nicolae Vogoride[174] had rigged the elections for the ad-hoc Convention. In a letter exchange with the Turkish embassy at London he set forth thoroughly his approaches against the unification of the two Romanian Principalities. The unionist intelligence service Alexandru Ioan Cuza[175] was part of among others, had intercepted the compromising letters of Vogoride◻s and published them in the French press, provoking not only an international scandal (France had issued threats of breaking diplomatic relations with the Ottoman Empire) but also the calling off of the elections.[XXXIV]

Several years later, in the perspective of an impending conflict with the Ottoman Empire over obtaining the state independency, the diplomatic missions of the United Principalities had been also sending data acquired from Vienna. For instance, in September 1876, the diplomatic representative at Rome, G. Cantacuzino, was conveying pieces of information over the stance of the great powers, procured at the Austria-Hungary embassy, based on "some secret annotations penned from Vienna by an influential person," therefore an informer, a "source" as called in the document.

Naturally, the Great Powers had been undertaking, too, such actions by means of agents, as it was the Austrian Friederich

Lachmann, dispatched at Bucharest under the cover of a press correspondent during the War of Independence[176], in fact for spying activities.

SPIES FOMENT REVOLT

Lately available documents have proved that besides social and economical reasons, some role in the breaking out of the 1907[177] peasant revolt from Romania had been played by the Austria-Hungary espionage and diversion agency, interested in undermining the situation from Romania with a view to expand its sphere of influence. For instance, such documents relate to infiltrating agents provocateur or public relation actions undertaken by way of some corrupted Romanian journalists. That's the reason why King Charles I of Romania[178] had interceded with Emperor Franz Joseph[179] for calling off such actions.

Several years later, the heads of some diplomatic missions of the Great Powers got embroiled in informative approaches over the Romanian territory. It is the case of the Austria-Hungary ambassador Count Ottokar Czernin (1872 – 1932), and the Germany ambassador, von dem Busche, both undertaking an intense spying activity by coordinating several operative and influence agents networks in Romania, aiming to determine Romania join the war on the side of the Central Powers (in the German original expression *Mittelmächte* – alliance formed by Germany, Austria-Hungary, the Ottoman Empire, as well as Bulgaria). In respect of Czernin, the close surveillance he had been subjected to led in 1914 to the appropriation of a briefcase comprising undeniable documents over the Austria-Hungary espionage activities in Romania, briefcase later on given back to him with formal "excuses." [XXXV]

In a similar manner there had been appropriated a briefcase belonging to the German Legation comprising lists of Romanian politicians and journalists to be recruited. Anyway, the head of the Austria-Hungary espionage, Maximilian Ronge, had later on admitted he had been dealt serious blows on behalf of the Romanian counter-information service, which proved to be an adversary to be reckoned with.

THE TREACHEROUS INVENTOR

In the history of the world aeronautics, the Romanian engineer and Lieutenant Rodrig Goliescu (1882 – 1942) had gone down as the inventor of "avioplane," the first flying craft with a tubular fuselage, whose first model was built in 1909. In the history of espionage Goliescu had gone down as that who in dire financial needs (probably over the expenses entailed by his invention) had dispatched to the Russians (though a middleman) some mobilization plans of the Romanian army. Arrested by the counter-espionage services, Goliescu would serve a 12 years term in penitentiary. On the mysterious circumstances of his death, the former inter-war Romanian prime minister Constantine Argetoianu[180] had written: *It looks like he died along with his mistress, poisoned by his wife who had also committed suicide.* [XXXVI]

THE LADY IN WHITE

For the first time in history, during the Great War the secret front could no more be told from the army confrontations. This entailed a reorganization of the intelligence services to face the global challenges related to the conflagration. This period brought along the superspies, of whom some were women, whose actions had more often than not borne a substantial influence on the events, or at least that was believed up to a given moment. Anyway, "the secret war" of spies had turned global, too.

Established in 1909, "Military Intelligence" (MI5)[181] was initially aimed to protect Great Britain against the infiltration of the German spies. At the same time it succeeded also in recruiting some spies that brought important contributions to the war effort of Great Britain. And the British espionage map had extended over most of the world, from the warring European states up to the Middle East.[XXXVII]

On the continent, the English espionage was mainly active in Belgium, where especially women agents like Louisa Cavell (1865 – 1915) had saved the lives of many Entente soldiers, only to end up herself in front of a firing squad. The spying activity of Juliette Hardy had incurred a real "sentimental drama," dying along with a German agent she had fallen in love with. Uncommonly active proved to be the "Lady in White" network where women agents standing out through a singular bravery, like Marie Birkel, had been part of.

EVERYTHING IN THE NAME OF HIS BRITISH MAJESTY

Though an ally of Great Britain, Russian had been a preferred target of the English espionage. One of the important agents proved to be Oswald Rayner (1889 – 1961), that who had seemingly shot to death the mystical faith healer Rasputin[182], suspected of having been German spy.

The East was one of the regions English espionage had been particularly active in, some of the masters of this field having been operating here. Thus was deemed Gertrude Margaret Lowthian Bell (1868 – 1926), an unusual personality, making allowance for her being the first woman with a degree in history at the Oxford University, and one of the first woman archeologist and intelligence officer. But certainly, one of the iconic and more sophisticated personality of that time, spy, archeologist and writer, had been the legendary Lawrence of Arabia, Thomas Edward Lawrence[183]. As a matter of fact, despite the important services he did to Great Britain, his activity was marred by bitter disappointments over his failing to establish an Arab state, as comes out from his volume "The Seven Pillars of Wisdom." Such disappointments Lawrence would experience, too, in consequence of his activities in India, penned down in other book of his, "Riot in the Desert."

But Great Britain was the first country to closely follow the example set by France in the Renaissance period, tapping the potential of intellectuals, writers, for informative and influence actions. Into the first category falls the playwright, novelist and critique Somerset Maugham (1874 – 1965), who had worked for the SIS intelligence service in Russia, where he tried unsuccessfully to win the benevolence of the provisional government headed by Kerensky[184] and induce Russia to remain in the Entente.[XXXVIII]

In 1914 there is founded the so called "War Propaganda Bureau" aiming to undertake propaganda and influence actions to the benefit of the political interests of Great Britain. From this structure, for long time secret, famous writers of English and universal literature like John Galsworthy[185], Joseph Rudyard Kipling[186], Arthur Conan Doyle[187] had been part of.

FROM CNOCKAERT TO ALOUETTE

French informative approaches in the war had been coordinated by the "Deuxième Bureau" as well as by the "National Security." Moreover, the tradition of women agents had been carried on by France during the First World War, too, these standing out through their performance, self denial and courage they had demonstrated. Working as nurse in a field hospital Marthe Cnockaert (1892 – 1969) had the opportunity to learn valuable pieces of information from the soldiers brought there, her encoded messages proving of real value for the French army.[XXXIX]

Louise de Bettingnies (1880 – 1918) was in charge of a very active informer network, and Marthe Richer ("Alouette"/ 1889 – 1949?) had been awarded, in consequence of her services as agent in few countries, the "Legion of Honor"[188]. Wishing to avenge her husband fallen on the front, Marthe Richer, of a ravishing beauty, went to captain Ladoux from the French military espionage "Deuxième Bureau" proposing him to become an agent. She is sent to Stockholm where was checked by Mata Hari[189] but had to leave the Swedish capital in a haste. Later on, in the summer of 1916, Richer is sent to Spain where she came into contact with the naval attaché of the German embassy in Madrid, von Krohn, who falls in love with her and agrees to dispatch false information meant to "intoxicate" the German espionage.

USA COMES INTO ACTION

The counter-informative activities of the United States had ramped up after entering into the war, materializing in the annihilation of many agents, more than 200, of Germany. Most of them had been… women! Nora Connolly - O⬚Brien had activated as spy for Germany in protest of the English policy in Ireland. The spying activity of Marie von Ladenburg sparked off a real scandal, being proved her having relations with the Great Britain ambassador himself.[XL]

„DEUTSCHLAND ÜBER ALLES UND MATA HARI"

Through the main espionage structure, the so called "IIIb", Germany had undertaken espionage activities all over the world in accordance with its aim to become a "Great power of espionage." Within this context, United States had been the country enjoying a close attention on behalf of the German espionage that had committed there some sabotage acts meant to prevent the country entering into the war and undermine later its war effort. One of the most efficient saboteurs proved to be Franz von Rintelen (1877 – 1949) and Franz Wachendorf.

German espionage had been active in France, too, where had acted Schluga von Rastenfeld (1841 – 1917), who managed to come by data from the French General Staff. The heads of German intelligence service deemed that agent as the most important phenomenon in the whole history of espionage, inasmuch as this history is known.[XLI]

*

An unusual attention had enjoyed the East, too, where Germany had attempted to counteract the authority of Great Britain and trigger riots of the local leaders. The most important German agent in that area was Wilhelm Wassmus (1880 – 1931). He set up a covert network handling, besides data acquiring, operative actions aiming to bring to an end Great Britain's and Russia's domination in the Middle East by setting off revolts, but he failed and went captured by the English.

Known more as "Miss Doctor" Elisabeth Schragmüller (1887 – 1940) had from many viewpoints "blazed a trail" in the espionage field of that time. After getting a doctorate she came to be one of the first women to head an intelligence service and also the only woman – officer from the German army. Schragmüller stands out as expert in interrogating deserters and prisoners of war. In 1915 she sets up in Anvers a school for the agent to be sent to France (one of her students was Mata Hari). The principles of the informative actions she had taught to her "students" would be used for a long time in the espionage schools.

If getting already to Mata Hari we ask ourselves the same question: who was she? The question might look superfluous, taking into account the wealth of literature on this super-spy. Under her real name Margaretha Geertruida Zelle (1876 – 1917), agent "H21" went down in history as the most important German spy in France and other countries. Even among the German officers there is no consensus over Zelle having been a spy with results to match the legend woven around her. French historian Paul Allard wrote in 1933: *I read all that had been written about the famous dancer Mata Hari and I am none the wiser. I don*t *know yet what Mata Hari had done,"* and the author of a world history of espionage J. Piekalkiewicz, says: *It is possible that the best known spy of all time to have had less* *success regarding her informative approaches than her Java temple dancer performances on stage.* Over her artistic qualities, even Zelle had stated that her only merit was that of having danced naked. The informative services historian Philip Knightley believes that after all "Z" (as fondly called) was nothing but a "scapegoat" of the military and political leaders of that time.[XLII]

THE EASTERN EUROPE ESPIONAGE IN THE GREAT WAR

During the First World War (1914 – 1918) the most successful informative activity in the Eastern Europe had been performed both by structures of the Romanian Army General Staff (MCG) and General Security and Police Directorate of Romania, having in its ranks many plainclothes agents and volunteers inspired by patriotic convictions.

Naturally, the success was possible due to both the diplomatic and secret services getting directly involved in (counter)-informative actions prior to the war and during it. On the one hand we talk about the diplomats getting engaged into the confrontations on the "secret front," both internal and external, and on the other hand counteracting the espionage activities undertaken by the Central Powers services on the country's territory. As a matter of fact, the faceoff between the two military intelligence services began even before the breaking out of the conflict between Austria-Hungary and Romania, right in the Austria-Hungary capital.

Thus, the Romanian secret service had managed even before Romania having entered into the war in 1916 to set up an informer network in the capital of the Empire, under the control of the Romanian ambassador, Mavrocordat, himself. An important contribution had had the military attaché of the Romania legation, captain Traian Starcea, his network being comprised of about 50 persons, among whom diplomats and foreign military attaches. Active within the network set up by Starcea had been other diplomats, too, as well as the commercial attaché Vasile Candini. It looks like the two had activated as double agents for other enemy states of Austria-Hungary. Most of the members of this network, among whom there were Romanian students in Vienna, had been arrested by the Austria-Hungary counterespionage, being released in 1918.XLIII

*

Another Romanian that stood out in this field had been Doctor Ion Nandris, who was picking information from the Romanians all over Austria-Hungary, in particular from those both around the Romanian Orthodox Chapel in Vienna and the army, which he was sending through Switzerland to Romania. Nandris himself was picking information from the "battlefield" by means of a forged passport.

As recorded by a contemporary of his, Doctor Octavian Lupu, Ion Nadris: *had been in that time the keenest and most fearless fighter of the irredentist movement from Vienna, making himself great sacrifices,* and adding*: To the great honor of that generation it can be said that either in Vienna or other lands there are no traitors among us.* But unluckily, as we▯ll see later on, they happened to be in Romania itself! As to Ion Nandris, having been in the end tailed he got away "as if by magic," seeking refuge in the countryside until de end of the war.

*   .

As a matter of fact, even before entering into the war, the Romanian espionage services had recruited a secret agency from the ranks of the Romanians on the territories belonging to the Austria-Hungary, agency that had provided valuable intelligence to the Romanian army in case of offensive operations. Within the General Headquarters there had been founded a special bureau to coordinate these actions. Once Romania entered into the war (August 14/27, 1916) the Romanian espionage had ramped up its activities. Maximilian Ronge, the head of the Austria-Hungary espionage, had admitted the important informative role the Romanian patriots had played during the Transylvania offensive: *The Romanian espionage service had found among the Transylvanian population, already stirred up by the nationalist agitators, many sympathizers...* Such actions led to many Romanians in the Austria-Hungary army deserting the colors.[XLIV]

Also worth noticing are the actions of the group led by Spiridon Boita in Brasov, consisting of over 200 persons, bearing the name "The Hanged Men Club", making allowance for the fact that if apprehended that would be punishment in store for them.

After Romania had entered into the war, the actions of the Romanian secret services, enjoying the large support of the population, made a critical contribution to the setting up of the defense at Marasesti[190].

*

Like other European intelligence services, the Romanian one, too, had called on "feminine espionage." One of these spies was Tereza Colbeu. On her arrest in the fur collar she was wearing there had been found informative documents. But the most important woman agent proved to be Maria Balan, who had dispatched for long many valuable pieces of information over the Austria-Hungary military units movements in Banat, activating under the code name "B9". The Austria-Hungary espionage encounters great difficulties in identifying the young and beautiful woman. Once arrested she is condemned to death but managed to escape and showed up in Bucharest. Of Balan, the French newspaper "Paris Soir" wrote she was "the queen of espionage", a local "Mata Mari" who "had provided great services to Romania."

*

Unfortunately, the Romanian counter-information service had to take on not only the external enemy but also the interior one. We mean the identifying and annihilation of some agents at the service of the Central Power espionage, sometimes acting from quite high positions. After all, their actions, spurred by large sums of money and other rewards, offices in a future occupied Romania, had taken a toll on the lives of some fellow countrymen.

At last, we have to remind the case of some Romanians who had spied in... Romania from their positions of servicemen in the Austria-Hungary army. For instance, we talk about Lieutenant Leo Onciul, who is taken prisoner by the Romanian Army, and after breaking loose sets forth a detailed report forwarded to the Austria-Hungary military authorities on the Romanian army.

Of the agents at the service of the Austria-Hungary espionage, the most important proved to be Colonel Victor Verzea, who from his position of head of postal services, even since the neutrality of Romania, had sent to the enemy, to the ambassador Czernin and the German one, the telegram decrypting code, copies of the correspondence of military commanders and politicians. Once the Central Powers troops had entered Bucharest he made available to them the telegraphic and postal installations. As reward for his services, Verzea is appointed by the occupation authorities mayor of Bucharest. In 1919, at Bucharest, there is pronounced a life imprisonment sentence, which would not be enforced because on November 9, 1920 the crimes perpetrated during the war, among which those of espionage, had been pardoned. [XLV]

THE INTER-WAR COLD WAR

Even since the inter-war period, United States became the main target of the soviet espionage carried out by the secret organizations NKVD/OGPU/GPU/KGB and the military agency GRU, in consequence of this country's political significance and the cutting edge technology that could be "purchased" thence. In particular there had been employed the method of setting up agent networks, members or sympathizers of the Communist Party, now in high positions in the American administration, who had acted as influence or operative agents for USSR.

Harold M. Ware (1890 – 1935) was the head of the network bearing his name and comprising persons from various ministries of the US administration (Department of Agriculture, Department of Justice, Department of the Interior) who had spied for USSR in the thirties. A staunch backer of collectivization in USSR, Ware works for a while in the Soviet Union, later on acting as agent and militant for the American economic assistance to the "Country of the Soviets." Of the many agents that had been part of "The Ware Network" there had been high dignitaries from the State Department (Foreign Office), Alger Hiss, Laurence Duggan, Noel Field, as well as other high ranking governmental clerks like Lee Pressman.

Whittaker Chambers (1901 – 1961), the most important liaison and courier in the inter-war period, had been part of the network led by Nathan Silvermaster, working at "The Board of Economic Warfare", position allowing his to convey to Soviet Union data of great importance on the armament production, naval and air forces of the USA. In 1938, disgruntled by the Soviet methods, Chambers splits with the Communist Party and denounces the network members activating in the USA.

Of the so called "Mocase Network" outstandingly active proved to be Jack Soble, Boris Morros (1891 – 1963), a complex agent who had carried out espionage actions for USSR and in Germany, France, Switzerland, Austria, Japan, Canada, turning in the end double agent and working for FBI, too. Naturally, most of these networks carried on and stepped up their activities during the Second World War, too.

*

The method of "the feminine espionage" had been used by the soviet agencies in the USA, too. There stood out of the crowd Martha Dodd (1908 – 1990), the daughter of the United States ambassador to Germany, whose case is unparalleled in history: the daughter spying on her father! Another unusual case was that of Juliette Stuart Poyntz (1886 – 1937), an American spy for USSR who, when Stalin unleashes "The Great Terror", shows the true colors of the soviet regime which she deems as "corrupt, criminal, unlawful", reason why she had been assassinated.[XLVI]

"THE SOVIET MAN" JACK LONDON

As a matter of course the American counterespionage didn't lie idle and undertook some measures, among which drawing up a list to include not only the persons suspected as American communist sympathizers or agents for USSR (the art collector Armand Hammer, writers Richard Nathaniel Wright, Jack London[191] – real name John Griffith Chaney) but from other countries too (Bertolt Brecht[192], Thomas Mann[193]). In case of some persons it was concluded the suspicions had been ungrounded but they had been maintained on the "FBI list" until post war years.

LAWRENCE OF MANCHURIA

The Great Power ambitions of Japan stood behind this state, too, having called on espionage against countries seen as potential future adversaries or targeted by the Japanese expansion. Thus, Yoshitaro Amana (1899 - ?) had operated within the so called "Tanaka Plan," a Japanese strategy of world domination – set forth by the Prime Minister Tanaka Giichi to Emperor Hirohito[194] in 1927, aiming also to undertake espionage actions with a view to lay ground for a USA invasion.[XLVII]

That called "Lawrence of Manchuria," Kenji Doihara, had set up a large spy network in China and had a major contribution in bringing to power the "puppet regime" of Manchukuo[195] (Manchuria) in 1932.

CHIANG KAI-SHEK DOES NOT FORGET

Due to its economic potential China had been targeted by the espionage actions of some Great Powers aiming to expand their influence over that huge region or conquer it. Soviet Union's intentions consisted in creating conditions for bringing to power a communist regime in China.

Marie Picard, who had picked information for USSR from the nationalist camp of Chiang Kai-Shek[196] ended up being executed upon his order. But there are some instances where the real name of the agent remained unknown. Among them is that who activated in the inter-war China under the codename "Mademoiselle Marie," dancer, "woman with a goddess body," agent for Great Britain, who brought at least for a while her contribution to foiling Moscow's plans of unleashing a revolt in China.

THE MEXICAN "RECIPE"

Mexico found its way on the informative actions map and political assassinations due to last "Trotsky case" episode having taken place there. The soviet dissident was seen by I.V. Stalin as his main enemy, so that he ordered the soviet espionage services to take him out. After several failed attempts NKVD recruits Ramon Mercader[197], of Spanish origin but a fiery communist.[XLVIII]

This, on August 20, 1940 seriously injures Leon Trotsky[198], who would later die. Mercader is set free in 1960 and arrives in USSR where he is awarded the title "Hero of the Soviet Union". His portrait is at the KGB museum from Moscow. Worth reminding is that the well known Mexican drawer David Alfaro Siqueiros (1896 – 1974) had been also involved in the assassination attempts against Trotsky.

ANOTHER KIND OF SECRET WORLD WAR

The secret front had superposed and sometimes went beyond the trench one, bearing every now and then a decisive influence on it. It can be said that one of the reasons the Allies, after having their ups and downs, had prevailed in the Second World War was them winning the "spy war," too. Understanding, after the First World War experience, that victory was to a large extent depending on informative, influence and sabotage actions, the states in the antifascist alliance had mobilized their forces, human and technological potential to win "the secret war." The edge they had consisted in the soldiers (agents, spies) on mission being motivated by knowing that the defense of democracy and even survival of the states against the totalitarian threat was depending on them.

It can be said that for most of the conflagration Great Britain had borne the brunt of the "secret war," realizing that removing the danger of the hostilities reaching its homeland and other regions of the world was depending on winning it on the continent.

*

Having a substantial experience and well trained agents and collaborators, the two agencies the British intelligence service was consisting of (MI5, MI6[199]) had operated through espionage approaches in several "hotspots" on the "war map," sometimes calling on methods of unparalleled cleverness.

For instance, that⊡s the case of diplomat John Lomax, nicknamed "The Tiger", who had set up the conveyance by devious routes, namely through other countries, in particular Spain and even USA, of the diamonds from the occupied region of France and the high precision mechanisms used in aviation industry from Switzerland to Great Britain. Amy Elizabeth Thorpe (1910 – 1963), the wife of the British ambassador to Washington, had also succeeded, by calling on her feminine charm, in getting from the Italian diplomats the navy codes of that country, used later during the Allied landing in North Africa.[XLIX] Furthermore, she had operated in Poland under the codename "Cynthia" and afterwards "Betty Pack," providing data on the Adolf Hitler⊡s decision to break up Czechoslovakia[200], helping likewise in decoding the Nazi Germany radio messages.

Another important mission had consisted in obtaining the communication codes of the pro-Nazi government at Vichy[201], thing achieved by seducing a member of the French diplomatic corps.

THE EMPLOYMENT OF DOUBLE AGENTS

Double agents had been successfully employed by the British SIS (Secret Intelligence Service or MI6). One of the most important proved to be the Yugoslavian Dusan/Dusko Popov (1912 – 1981), the model agent 007 had been inspired of. Recruited by the military intelligence service of Nazi Germany ("Abwehr") he also proffers his collaboration to the intelligence service of Great Britain, which agrees on Popov becoming double agent. He delivers credible but doctored information by this agency, keeping up his credibility to "Abwehr." In exchange he learns from the Germans consequential strategic data for England, already engaged in war. Activating in the USA, too, Popov comes by data over the Japanese interest in the naval base at Pearl Harbor[202] and the impending Japanese onslaught, but the head of FBI, J. Edgar Hoover[203] does not inform his superiors out of reasons still unclear.[L]

In 1940, when it dawned on Great Britain that the war would be long and having to be waged by all available means, the informative, espionage and diversion ones included, Prime Minister Winston Churchill had decided to establish "Special Operations Executive" (SOE). Its mission was to back espionage and sabotage actions behind enemy lines, shaping up a core of the future auxiliary units having to get into action in case of a German invasion. Under the orders of this agency there had been 13,000 agents, and those about one million operations it had supported and set up had been carried out over all the war operation theaters from Europe and Asia.[LI] Of the SOE members we remind Forest Frederick Edward Yeo-Thomas (1901 – 1964), who is often parachuted in France where he is active in organizing the Resistance movement. Another one, the Norwegian scientist Leif Hans Larsen Tronstad (1903 – 1945) succeeds in gaining data on the production of V2[204] missile by the Germans at Peenemünde, leading to the bombing of the factory by the Allied air forces.

THE WOMEN SPY COMMUNITY

Most of the SOE agents had been women, standing out through their cleverness and self denial, sometimes paying the ultimate price for their courage. The organizer of the women spy section from SOE had been Vera Maria Atkins, regarded *as the most important secret agent in the Second World War.* Vera had been born on June 16, 1908 in Galati (a Danube harbor) and had distinguished herself by being fluent in English, French, Romanian and German. Her real name was Maria Vera Rosenberg, Atkins being the maiden name of her mother who fled the pogroms in Russia. Her father, Max Rosenberg, Jewish financier and businessman, born in Germany, had enjoyed success in Romania and amassed a huge fortune. In the thirties he ended up advising the Romanian King Carol II on financial matters.

The author of the James Bond series, the writer and former spy Ian Fleming[205], who was personally acquainted with Vera Atkins since working both for the British Special Operation Service, got inspired by her personality in making up the character Moneypenny, the superior of His Majesty super-agent, the famous 007.

The mission of Vera consisted both in setting up resistance over the German occupied territory, sabotage and terrorist attacks against German war machine (blowing up bridges and trains) as well as picking up information. Atkins had airdropped   men,   ammunitions,   weapons   and   radio transmitters to lay ground for D Day, the landing in Normandy.

In 1987, the government in Paris had awarded Vera Atkins the high distinction of *the Legion of Honor* for her entire activity of coordinating and supporting French resistance movement and her contribution to liberating France from under German occupation.

One of the most important SOE woman agents that had activated on the continent was Virginia Hall, "the most dangerous of the Allied woman spies," the India origin Noor Inayat Khan (1914 – 1944), Odette Sanson (1912 – 1995), Krysztyna Skarbek (1908 – 1952), who can be deemed as the spy activating over the largest area, including several countries from Africa and Europe, Violette Szabo (1921 – 1945), who had carried out many sabotages against German army, Elizabeth P. McIntosh, who had activated in the East, the author of the volume "Sisterhood of Spies."[LII]

JAMES BOND... IS BORN!

The Second World War, which led to an unprecedented flare up of informative activities on both sides, paved the way for a more direct involvement of some writers, several of global renown, in setting up and carrying out espionage actions.

Unusual is some of these writers having been promoted to executive positions in the intelligence services, acquiring thus data to be later used in devising espionage novels, genre gaining much popularity after the war. A particular situation is the agent career of Graham Greene[206]. After proffering his services to a representative of the German espionage he activates as SIS agent on some "war theaters" to be later found in his novels, afterwards siding with Kim Philby[207], one of the most important agents of USSR and Fidel Castro☒s[208] regime. But the most famous are the diversion and spying methods made up by Ian Lancaster Fleming (1908 – 1964), as subtle as those in his James Bond novels.

*

At the same time, the British intelligence services had to set in motion a real spy "hunting" on their own territory.[LIII] It may look strange, but besides apprehending some German spies as it was Vera Chalbur (1912 - ?), there had been fingered spies at the service of the Great Britain☒s ally, USSR: the cases of financiers Nathaniel Rothschild (1910 – 1990) and Arthur Wynn (1910 – 2001), both acting to recruit agents among college students.

THE DIABOLICAL BASTIEN...

Most of the French espionage and sabotage actions had been carried out on its own German occupied territory within the Resistance movement in its showdown with the powerful agencies of "Gestapo"[209] and "Abwehr". And that seen as leader of the Resistance movement, Jean Moulin (1898 – 1943), had to undertake informative and sabotage actions as well as intelligence gathering on German army. After having been airdropped over France he makes contact and coordinates several groups that had carried out such actions (like "Combat" or "Armée secrète"). He is apprehended after being betrayed by an infiltrated woman agent and dies in captivity.[LIV]

The well known dancer, actress and singer Josephine Baker[210], after having been given French citizenship in 1939 had offered to collaborate with the French counter-intelligence services, her task being to pick up data during the tournaments performed in Germany, occupied France and other countries. Of great importance proved to be the intelligence on the fortifications built by the government in Vichy against the Allied landing in Europe. In recognition of her achievements Baker had been awarded diverse orders and medals, being the first American woman to be awarded "Croix de la Guerre."

... "AND THE CAT"

At opposite poles had been two woman agents that proved to be especially detrimental to the Resistance movement, playing an important role in the apprehension of some of its members. Infiltrated by the Gestapo among the people leading the Resistance, Lydie Bastien (1922 – 1993) betrays Jean Moulin. After liberation Bastien tries her hand at unlawful activities, getting the nickname "The diabolical one." She died poisoned, probably by one of her confederates.

On the other side, after getting captured by the Gestapo, Mathilde Carre (1908 – 1970), nicknamed "The cat," agrees to become double agent. The information she provided to the Germans led to the dismantling of some Resistance networks.

Worth noticing, though France was on the same side with USSR, the soviet espionage had recruited several agents, among them the politician Pierre Cot (1895 – 1977), exposed after the war, and Jacques Duclos (1896 – 1975) himself, the leader of the French Communist Party, who had provided USSR information about the French military potential. After the war he was exposed and placed under temporary arrest.[LV]

OPERATION ENORMOZ

Besides its war effort, Soviet Union, through its main agencies GPU, OGPU, NKVD, GRU, had been in particular likewise active on the secret front, not only against the Allies⊠ adversaries but them too, especially United States, where technological data acquiring, mostly on the atomic bomb, has been initiated. Over the territory of that state the soviet agents had acted in particular under diplomatic immunity, their main goal being gaining data on the atomic bomb production "Manhattan Project" ("Operation Enormoz").

One of the most "successful" of those "atomic spies" proved to be Grigori Heifetz (? – 1953), who comes into contact with scientist working on that project, among whom Bruno Pontecorvo and Robert Oppenheimer. Anatoli Antonovici Iatskov (1913 – 1993) was the head of an "atomic spies" network. Mikhail Mukassei (1907 – 2008) along with his wife activates in the American "film citadel," Hollywood, befriending actors, directors and famous writers (Theodore Dreiser[211], Charlie Chaplin[212], Walt Disney[213]).[LVI] Haik Badalovici Ovakimian (1898 – 1967) recruits the Rosenbergs, due to which he was appointed in 1939 head of the soviet technical scientific espionage in the USA.

Julius Rosenberg was born on May 12, 1918 and Ethel Greenglass on September 28, 1915 in New York. Both had joined The Communist Youth League in the United States in 1936. They got married three years later and had two sons

Robert and Michael Rosenberg. After their parents had been put to death, the children went adopted by Abel and Anne Meeropol.

David Greenglass, Ethel's brother, had joined "Manhattan Project," regarding the development of the first American atomic bomb, in Los Alamos (New Mexico). The data had been passed on to the counter-information service of the soviet army, the famous Glavnoie Razvedîvatelnoie Upravlenie (GRU).

In 1950, within "VENONA" project, the atomic physicist Klaus Fuchs, of German origin, had been exposed as soviet spy. The inquiry revealed that David Greenglass and the Rosenbergs respectively had been participating in sending the information to the soviets. Project VENONA had been a joint approach of the American intelligence services and British MI6 aiming to identify and decode messages conveyed from and to the soviet intelligence services.

THE NUCLEAR NETWORK

In Great Britain, under diplomatic immunity, Anatoli Veniaminovici Gorski (1907 – 1980), handles the spies from "The Cambridge Group" and those working on penetrating the atomic bomb project, like Iury Modin.

Lately there had come out several diaries of a high ranking MI5 official, providing us an entrancing image over the cold war espionage activities.

The ten diaries belong to the MI5 deputy chief executive Guy Liddell, and date back to the early period of the conflict between the west and soviet camps. In his diaries Liddell had written extensively on his relations with the British government, other key figures of the British espionage, as well as about the famous spy group at Cambridge he had good views on before revealing their double game.

According to the pundits, Liddell's diaries, resuming a series of diaries discontinued by the breaking out of the war, can provide a significant contribution to understanding that period by coming from a high ranking source having access to classified information.

Liddell diaries provide also details on what happened in MI5 when Donald Maclean and Guy Burgess, two of the double agents at Cambridge, fled Great Britain. Liddell wrote then *it looks highly unlikely to me that such a brilliant man as Burgess had ever thought of having a future in Russia.* Regarding these double agents, Liddell's diaries supply yet unknown information: for instance, Kim Philby, one of the Cambridge Five, who in 1950 was in Washington as MI6 agent, had attempted to have Liddell appoint him MI5 agent, too.

Liddell depicts also the moment the MI5 agents had informed their superiors that the soviets had run a successful test of an atomic bomb. He recounts that the Foreign Office representative, William Hayter, after having urged the secretaries to leave, had warned those present there they had better step out of the room if unable to keep for themselves what they would be told. The findings baffled everyone and turned their plans upside down, wrote Liddell on New Year's Eve in 1950, not yet sure whether the bomb was but experimental or the soviets had indeed the real one. Anyway, he was writing "there's no doubt that until 1967 the soviets will have enough atomic bombs to wipe out entirely this country."

Some experts believe the Russians could gain at least one year in the development of their atomic weapons than initially thought due to the information passed on by the physicist Klaus Fuchs then residing in Great Britain. He is referred to several times in the Liddell's diaries, his also writing about the method Fuchs called on when setting up secret meetings with the Russians: he had to toss a magazine marked at page 10 into a given London garden, and his liaison with the Russians was to let him a chalk written message on a lighting post.

The scandal that broke out after Fuchs was exposed led to a temporary straining of the relations between England and USA, the Americans being mad about the information leaks. In 1950, a Liddell on the edge was writing that *the Americans are utterly unable to grasp any other viewpoints than theirs!*

But the soviets do not sleep! Nikolai Zabotin, too, acts in Canada setting up a network aiming to gain atomic secrets as long as that country too had joined the atomic bomb project.

THE LONG JUMP OF ESPIONAGE

In Germany, Nikolai Ivanovici Kuznetov (1911 – 1944) operates under the identity of a German officer, passing on data of great significance over the German onslaught at Kursk and the production of V2 missiles.[LVII] A legendary figure of the soviet espionage, posthumously awarded the order "Hero of the Soviet Union," Kuznetov is the spy who got the first information on the "Operation Long Jump," a plan aiming to assassinate the leaders of the Allied countries participating at the Tehran conference (November 28 – December 1, 1943).

On the other hand, though declared "Hero of the Soviet Union," the identity of Gevork Andreevici Vartanian (1924 - ?) had been kept secret until 2000. He was that who used the data provided by Kuznetov on the "Operation Long Jump" to foil it. Vartanian had laid bare the "Operation Long Jump" plans and prevented thus it being carried out.

THE FUHRER, KEEN ON CHEKOV

Actress Olga Chekova (1897 – 1980), nephew of the great writer Anton Chekov[214], called "the uncrowned queen of the soviet espionage," managed to come into contact with some high ranking officials of the Third Reich, her main goal being passing on information about the German offensive plans against Soviet Union. Journalist Mark Steinberg wrote in the Russian publication "Nezavisimaia Gazeta" that during the Nazi tenure Olga had conveyed successfully important data to Moscow.

Under her real name Olga Leonardovici Kipper, she was born into a family of "Russified" Germans. In the beginning that bore no significance. But later on, when Olga – in the meantime turned into a cherished actress of MXAT (The Moscow Artistic Theatre) – would arrive to Germany, her origin would play an important role. Olga had mingled singe child with the Russian aristocracy, while seen in adolescence as a ravishing beauty.

Of those hooked by her irresistible charms was a nephew of Chekov's, Mikhail. They got married in 1914, and their union "had lasted" six years. Mikhail Chekov was appreciated in Moscow, as artist being deemed later on as one of the greatest actors and directors of the XX century. At a given moment he left for Germany, then France, England and USA. His only love would forever bear from then on the name Olga.

One year after the divorce Olga would marry a director, until then unknown, the Hungarian Ferencz Iarosi. In 1922 they would go together to the West but afterwards something happened. The actress would be summoned to the Soviet Military Headquarters and forced under pressure to work for an espionage agency abroad. All of a sudden Olga went on a visit to Germany to see an aunt of hers, Chekov's wife respectively.

What's interesting is that Ferencz, Olga's husband, would never know anything about the second "avocation" of his spouse. Her acting career would not be affected, on the contrary, proving more glamorous and successful, in particular to the male public. She began to be looked for by theater directors and film producers. She would play in some of the best Berlin theaters and shoot a lot: from frivolous, even erotic parts to composition roles. The critiques agreed upon Olga being entrancing and brilliantly talented both as prostitute and aristocrat.

Olga wasted no time and became the closest friend of Hitler's mistress, Eva Braun[215]. By way of her she would get acquainted with Adolf, to turn eventually into the greatest admirer of hers. The dictator would even decree the establishment of a special "order" for her, "Actress of the Reich." He knew she was German, this thing playing an important role in their public and private relations. For many times Hitler had proposed her to change the name she kept from her first husband, Mikhail Chekov, on the ground that he was Jew by his maternal line. But Olga was adamant in her refusal.

Thus, as soviet spy, she enjoyed unseen before opportunities to gain access to top secret documents. Her sources? The easiest to get to: high ranking officials of the Reich and the Fuhrer himself.

In particular relative to an important leader of the Nazi regime, Marshall Hermann Goering[216], Olga behaves in a special manner. His wife was likewise an actress, and worth noticing, the spy's best friend!

Many biographers had attempted to shed light on the Fuhrer's attraction to that Chekova. Some blamed it on Hitler's "sexual anomalies." Some pieces of information in this respect come out from an autobiographic book of Olga's, published in Munich in 1973. In this book Olga runs fragments from Eva Braun's diary. Eva writes that in case the intellectual level of his partner was below a certain standard Hitler was forcing her into sexual perversions. That situation even Eva had been in. But it looks like Olga had been a special partner for him due to her intellectual qualities. Anyway, the German women were seeing him, according to the testimonies of that time, "polite, charming, stylish and very handsome." Probably his hypnotic eyes were inspiring many of them a fatal attraction.

After having been deemed in the late Twenties as the best actress of Germany, in the summer of 1944 she ran the risk of being exposed. Gestapo got her in their sight but lacked solid evidence. She talked to Hitler and the Gestapo got the message. Olga would be arrested on April 27, 1945 by soviet officers, but she called her "friends" from Moscow and the situation was worked out through a hasty flight to Moscow.

Her life in Moscow proved to be not unlike that in Germany: interviews with Beria[217] – the head of NKVD (The People☐s Commissariat for Internal Affairs) several brief visits to Kremlin topped by appointments with Stalin himself – who would award her the "Lenin" order. In 1949 Olga settles casually in West Berlin. In time he had given many interviews attempting to parry the charges of having collaborated with the soviet secret services. Moreover, in the West there came out several books where Olga is called "the uncrowned queen of the soviet espionage" or "that Mata Hari of the Red Empire." "The Queen" died in 1980, aged 83, from a brain tumor.

SORGE, TURNED DOWN BY STALIN AFTER HAVING SAVED USSR

However, by and large, the most important personality of the Japanese and Soviet espionage was Richard Sorge (in Russian *Рихард Зорге*), revolutionary, journalist and high class spy of Soviet Union in Japan, before and during the Second World War. His NKVD codename was "Ramsay."

Richard Sorge was born on October 4, 1895 in Baku, Azerbaijan, province of the Tsarist Empire in that time. He was one of the nine children of Wilhelm Sorge, German mining engineer, and his Russian wife Nina. The family moved to Germany when Richard was only three years old. His uncle was an associate of Karl Marx[218].

In October 1914 Sorge had volunteered to fight in the First World War. He was posted to a field artillery battalion for students. In March 1916 he was severely wounded when a shrapnel broke both his legs and left him limping for life. He was promoted to the rank of corporal and awarded the "Iron Cross"[219], and later on medically discharged.

During his convalescence he read Marx and became a Communist. He spent the rest of the war studying economics at the universities of Berlin, Kiel and Hamburg. Sorge received a doctorate in political sciences. He joined the German Communist Party (KPD), reason why he was laid off from both a teaching job and coal mining work. He went to Moscow where he joined Comintern[220] and became an agent for that organization.

In 1921 Richard Sorge returned to Germany, married Christiane Gerlach and moved to Solingen. In 1922 the communists had dispatched him to Frankfurt am Main where he began collecting data on the business community. After a failed communist coup attempt in the Ruhr industrial area, he took to working as journalist.

In 1924 he moved to Moscow where he officially became member of the Comintern International Liaison Department, another covert espionage service of OGPU. Despite accommodating his wife at "Lux Hotel" and giving her large amounts of money, due to his overworking penchant he ended up divorcing. In 1928 he became member of GRU, and in 1930 was sent to Shanghai to gather intelligence and foment revolution. Officially he was working as editor of the German news section of "Frankfurter Zeitung." Here he met Ozaki Hozumi, a Japanese journalist working for "Asahi Shimbun." In January 1932 he covered the fights between Chinese and Japanese on the streets of Shanghai. In December 1932 he was summoned back to Moscow, where he was decorated and remarried.

In 1933 he was transferred to Berlin under the codename "Ramsay" ("Рамзай" - Ramzai) to restore his contacts in Germany to be sent later on as representative of a Nazi newspaper in Japan. He reached Yokohama on September 6, 1933.

Between 1933 – 1934 Richard Sorge had set up in Japan an intelligence network to the benefit of NKVD. His agents had contacts with important politicians and through them to information over Japanese foreign policy. He resumed his ties with Ozaki Hozumi, an intimate of the Prime Minister (Prince) Fumimaro Konoye. Ozaki had copied secret documents for Richard Sorge.

Richard Sorge had officially joined the Nazi Party and collaborated as "Abwehr" agent with the embassy and the German ambassador Eugene Ott. He used the embassy to double check the information. During that time he took up drinking heavily.

Richard Sorge had provided to the soviets critical data on the Anti-Comintern Pact as well as on the German-Japanese Pact, and also warned about the attack at Pearl Harbor. In 1941 Sorge had informed his soviet superiors about the date "Operation Barbarossa" would be unleashed. Moscow thanked him but did next to nothing to counteract the German onslaught.

Prior to the Battle of Moscow Sorge had dispatched the crucial information about the Japanese not attacking Soviet Union in the Far East. This essential information allowed Jukov to move the military units deployed in Siberia to the Capital to bolster the defense and prepare the counterattack.

The second crucial information provided by Richard Sorge concerned the defense of Stalingrad. The unusually efficient spy alerted the soviets about the Japanese attacking USSR as soon as the German would seize any important city on the

Volga. Thus, the German victory would have meant cutting off the oil supply from Baku and the Allied shipment of ammunitions and food through the vital route crossing the Persian Gulf – Iran – Azerbaijan and River Volga.

Thus, the Japanese secret services had intercepted many of the messages sent by Sorge and began to tighten the noose around him. Ozaki had been arrested on October 14, 1941 and interrogated. Richard Sorge had been arrested on October 18, 1941 in Tokyo but had not been exchanged with Japanese prisoners of war because both the soviet government and Sorge had denied his having spied for USSR. He had been sent to the Sugamo prison.

Richard Sorge had been hanged on November 7, 1944 (10:20 AM), Ozaki being hanged on the same day. Soviet Union had formally acknowledged the services of Sorge but two decades later, on the ground that Stalin could not afford to be found out that he had overlooked the information over the date of 1941 German invasion of USSR. Thus, on November 5, 1964 Richard Sorge had been posthumously decorated with the highest distinction "Hero of the Soviet Union."

In 1961 there had been shot in France a French – West German – Italian – Japanese coproduction titled "Qui êtes-vous, Monsieur Sorge?" ("Who are you Mister Sorge?"). The movie was well received in the Soviet Union, too.

Cold War classified documents alleged that Richard Sorge had not been executed but secretly handed over by the

Japanese to the soviets, his carrying on working for KGB. However, after the falling of communism in USSR there had emerged no credible evidence to back this theory. Anyway, as Ian Fleming, too, the father of the famous James Bond, said: "Richard Sorge was the most formidable spy in history."

MULTIPLE AGENTS

Special mission agents had been those soviet spies who had operated in more countries, being assigned multiple tasks. One of these was Pavel Anatolievici Sudoplatov (1907 – 1996). During the Second World War Sudoplatov was in charge of a special unit setting up assassinations and sabotages against the German troops.

In 1941 Pavel Sudoplatov is appointed head of "Department S," integrating elements from NKVD and GRU, with a view to gather intelligence on the atomic bomb production, while after war getting engaged in sabotages against the Western countries. His autobiography, "Special Tasks" provides, inter alia, data on the scientists involved in the "Manhattan Project" who offered pieces of information on the atomic bomb production, some of them controversial.

Among the most important tasks of his were the assassination of Lev Davidovich Trotsky (an important politician in the first years of Soviet Union, later on People's Commissary for Foreign Affairs and then founder and first chief of the Red Army and People's Commissary for Defense). As aforementioned, among the tasks of Sudoplatov was finding out the secrets of atomic bomb by way of renowned scientists like Oppenheimer and Bohr.

Sudoplatov was the elite spy that knew the real role played by the Rosenbergs in the atomic espionage activities of USSR, the reason why Stalin had made up the "Physicians

Plot" and the "Zionist Conspiracy," who had ordered the execution of the Polish officers in the Katyn Forest, how Khrushchev, the successor of Stalin, and his confederates had planned the arrest and shooting of Beria.

Sudoplatov had been arrested in 1953 after the falling of Beria. Despite the tortures he was subjected to and utter isolation from prison he refused to "confess." Set free after 15 years he was rehabilitated only in 1992, helped by his son, Anatoly, professor of economics at the Moscow University.

TO THE MUSIC OF RED ORCHESTRA

The "Red Orchestra," designation given by Gestapo ("Rotte Kapelle"), is an umbrella term relating to various spy groups active on behalf of the allied states in the territories occupied by the Third Reich during the Second World War. The most important group was mainly acting for USSR, in particular by sending valuable information gathered from Germany, France, Holland and Switzerland. 117 members of the "Red Orchestra," among whom women, had been arrested by the Gestapo, most of them being decapitated.

In Germany the most important agents were Arvid Harnack (1901 – 1942), who along with his wife, Mildred, dispatch vital information over Germany's war economy, in particular energy resources, allowing thus USSR asses the oil reserves the Reich armored vehicles could rely on. Among the members of "Red Orchestra" in Germany were officers, too, like Harro Schulze-Boysen. Lately it was thought that one of the "Red Orchestra" sources in Germany was... Martin Bormann[221] himself!

In France and Belgium, the most important agent and coordinator of the network was Leopold Trepper ("The Big Boss"/ 1904 – 1982), who in spite of the services he had provided after the war was briefly imprisoned in Lubianka.

In Switzerland the head of the network was Rudolf Roessler ("Lucy"/ 1897 – 1962), who had gathered intelligence on "Operation Barbarossa" the German invasion of Soviet

Union, information Stalin had waved away. Important roles had been played by Alexander Rado (1899 – 1981), journalist and geographer, and Alexander Foote (1905 – 1956) respectively, who operates as double agent. In the end, upon German pressures, the Helvetian authorities hold in custody some of the "Red Orchestra" members. Though having provided important services to the Allies, after the war Rado had been condemned in USSR for... espionage!!![LVIII]

OSS AND ONI

In the United States of America, only after the founding of the Office of Strategic Services (OSS) in 1942, therefore only after the country had entered into the war, USA gets directly involved into the "secret war." OSS's responsibilities consisted in gathering intelligence on the activities of the foreign espionage agencies and preventing sabotages in the USA.[LIX]

As to their own espionage actions, it's again worth reminding the engagement of a writer, the great novelist Ernst Hemingway,[222] who had acted on behalf of the Office of Naval Intelligence (ONI). He embarks on a long voyage through Pacific, gathering intelligence over an impending Japanese attack against USA and sets up a flotilla of small boats not to miss the "submarine war" Germany wished to wage.

Before being appointed head of CIA (1953), during the Second World War Allan Dulles[223] had activated as OSS resident, being involved in several informative and "diplomatic espionage" actions.

"ANGEL" WALLENBERG

The Swedish diplomat Raoul Wallenberg (1912 – 1947) had been sent to Hungary upon the recommendation of USA's Office of Strategic Services (OSS) whose agent he became. He was provided with large amounts of money used to save from death over 30.000 (according to other sources more than 100.000) Hungarian Jews. In fact, as suggested by the title of a book on him ("The Angel Himself Has Spied") he undertook informative actions, too, in Hungary, reason why Wallenberg got arrested at the end of the war by the NKVD.[LX]

Besides gathering information about his spy activity the soviets wanted to use him in the talks with Sweden. As Wallenberg was refusing any kind of collaboration he "vanishes," being transferred to different camps and prisons and in the end most probably taken out.

OPERATION PASTORIUS

The American counterespionage had acted both against the German agents and "networks" from the interior, and some native-born spies at the service of foreign powers. George John Dasch (1903 – 1992) should have been part of one of these networks, who along with other agents (Ernest Peter Burger, Heinrich Harm Heink, Richard Quirin) is disembarked from a submarine on Long Island (New York) within "Operation Pastorius," envisaging carrying out sabotage and espionage actions over the US territory, in particular against railroads and armament industry. Dasch, who was in fact disgruntled with the Nazi regime, turns himself in to FBI and provides information about the other members of the network, who are arrested and sentenced to death. [LXI]

GOLOS NETWORK

Another field of action for OSS an FBI was undertaking intelligence gathering activities in the country by way of Americans in high administrative positions. Most of them were part of the networks which had worked for the Russian "ally," networks set up as aforementioned after the war.

As a matter of fact, most of the agents had been exposed after the war during "Operation Venona" where the encoded communications of the USSR[LXII] embassy had been surveyed. Thus, diplomat Alger Hiss (1904 – 1996) had informed on the outcome of few important international conferences, Dumbarton Oaks 1944 and San Francisco 1945, setting forth UN Charter[224]. But there had been also found agents inside OSS, like Maurice Hyman Halperin (1906 – 1995) from the Golos Network, which had provided the soviet espionage intelligence from all over the world, in particular diplomatically related.

THE QUEEN OF THE RED ESPIONAGE

Called "the queen of the red espionage," Elisabeth Bentley (1906 – 1963) collaborates with some of the most important agents for USSR living in the USA. She was gathering intelligence by way of communists and sympathizers working in departments and institutions of great strategic importance. This intelligence was passed on through the soviet residents, those regarding the economic and military potential of Germany, as well as the US preparations in case of a possible war against The Third Reich.[LXIII]

In 1945, Bentley reports to New Haven FBI office, saying she wanted to testify about her espionage activities for USSR. Her confessions sounded like the shock waves of a bomb. In accordance with them, no less than 150 persons, of whom 37 federal employees, had spied for USSR. However, it unexpectedly looks like the USSR agent holding the highest position was the President F. D. Roosevelt's[225] advisor, Harry Lloyd Hopkins (1890 – 1946). Being the main "intelligence source" in respect of the relations with USSR, Hopkins bore a particular influence on the President, making him believe in the good intentions of Stalin's. Some initiatives of Hopkins over USSR had later on raised suspicions, as for instance delivering data and materials required for producing an atomic bomb. As came out from "Operation Venona" and the testimonies of former KGB officers, Hopkins had activates as agent for USSR.

ROOSEVELT AND CHURCHIL HAD SMOKED... KENT

The most important American agent for Germany was the diplomat Gatewood Kent (1911 – 1988), who had passed on to "Abwehr" documents of great importance relating mostly to the correspondence between US President Franklin Delano Roosevelt and the British Prime Minister Winston Churchill.

*

On the other hand, as aforementioned, gaining the "atomic secrets" referring to the production of nuclear weapons within "Manhattan Project" had been the main task of the soviet espionage in the United States, these providing Moscow the possibility to level the balance of global politics and accede to the status of "Great Power." Against this background it is worth noticing that Operation Enormoz, so little written and talked about, as this approach was called, proved mostly successful by provided USSR a technological head start and "saving" it huge amounts of money needed for the development of the atomic bomb. [LXIV]

The first agent to pass on to USSR the atomic bomb plan was Ted Hall (1925 – 1999) but other atomic spies, too, most of them directly involved in "Manhattan Project", had had a special contribution in this sense. Thus, the German origin scholar, previously written about as having worked at Los Alamos, Klaus Fuchs, otherwise "an outstanding scientist," had provided, out of strictly ideological reasons, the soviet espionage hundreds of pages comprising theoretical data on the project and concrete methods of implementing it, in fact the outcome of the tests carried out. May Allan Nunn (1912 – 2003) had conveyed important data on the atomic explosion at Hiroshima and samples of uranium.

DID "THE FATHER" OF ATOMIC BOMB BETRAY?

The greatest earthquake was triggered by the news from 1945 referring to "the father of atomic bomb", Robert J. Oppenheimer (1904 – 1967), being denied the access to "classified information" in this field for having provided the soviet espionage a string of secret data. An important role in taking that decision was played by his being a communist sympathizer and having had relations with a soviet agent, Elisabeta Zarubina. Soviet agent Pavel Sudoplatov says that Oppenheimer had been one of the soviet atomic espionage "sources" under the codename "Star." Later on even KGB denied that the American atomic scientist had been agent, asserting his being but "a friend of USSR." The sanctions against Oppenheimer had been lifted but the suspicions still linger on.

Bruno Pontecorvo (1913 – 1993) had been "another atomic spy" for USSR, situation confirmed eventually by his refuge to Moscow. But the case of the Rosenbergs was by far the most spectacular of "the atomic spies" for having been the subject of a Moscow orchestrated international protest campaign against their sentence to death. However, the sentence had not been abated, evidence that the United States was unwilling to make concessions over such an important field as "the atomic espionage." But it was already too late…[LXV]

CICERO, PAID WITH COUNTERFEITED MONEY

Having under control many intelligence services, among which the Wehrmacht's "Abwehr" stood out regarding espionage while "Gestapo" and other police structures as to the counter-information activities, Germany early in the war was leading on "the secret front" but slowly it was left behind by the Allies services, in particular when working together.

Some of the most important agents of Nazi Germany were of other nationalities, being either recruited or providing their services out of material reasons. That's for instance the case of the Turk Elyesa Bazna (1904 – 1970) who, as valet of the Great Britain ambassador to Ankara, from October 1943 had been photographing secret documents within the mission, sent later on in exchange of large amounts of money (he was the best paid spy in history until then) to an attaché of the German embassy, Ludwig Moyzisch, who gave him the codename "Cicero" due to the eloquence of the intelligence provided. Not small was Bazna's surprise when he realized after the war that the bills he was paid with had been "produced" by Operation Bernhard, aiming to undermine the English economy through circulating counterfeited currency. LXVI

Worth remembering, the English had learned about Bazna by way of "Dusko" Popov, the famous spy having exposed the activity of "Cicero" thus that the British counterespionage could flood the "Abwehr" with information fabricated in its offices from London.

OPERATION BERNHARD

Less than a month after the invasion of Poland, important cadres from "Schutzstaffel" (SS) and The Reich Main Security Office (RSHA) met in Berlin in the building of the Finance Ministry to debate a proposal forwarded by the (SS) Major Alfred Naujocks. After seeking the advice of prominent financiers they drafted an ambitious plan aiming to destabilize the British economy.

The talks set as main objective counterfeiting Bank of England notes. As Reinhard Heydrich[226], the head of RSHA, was telling the SS Major Alfred Naujocks, those copies had to be replicas as good as possible of the originals thus that not even an expert could tell them apart. The next stage required a substantial contribution on behalf of "Luftwaffe," the Nazi air force, which had to deploy many of its aircrafts to drop counterfeited money over the United Kingdom.

Once circulated, the notes would have given a good shake to the British economy due to the uncontrolled inflation triggered by them. The low value of currency would have led to a deep economic crisis, the United Kingdom turning thus into an easy prey for The Third Reich.

German chancellor Adolf Hitler had been informed on this and agreed with the operation to carry on. However, there had been doubts raised within prominent members of the National Socialist Party (NSDAP), Joseph Goebbels, the minister of Public Enlightenment calling it "a grotesque plan" (*einen grotesken plan*) for the easy way it could be turned against Germany.

Inquisitive, Churchill had asked himself, not in the know of the German plan, if the Nazi regime could be brought down by ruining its economy. He is assured such an action would be doomed while they would have even been laughed at for envisaging it. Roosevelt, the American president, had been suggested something in this vein and when asking the opinion of his English counterparts he learns in amazement they had already turned down such option.

In spite of the secrecy surrounding the Nazi meeting the British espionage network had learned in due time about the plan and warned the Bank of England. The board of that institution deemed the counterfeiting of the banknotes impossible, but took preventive measures by forbidding the introduction of pounds in the country during the war.

In the first stage the action had been coordinated by Albert Langer, within "Operation Andreas," enjoying the backing of RSHA. The first hurdles were encountered in the German laboratories when attempting to replicate exactly the paper used for printing the English pounds, and the lack of expertise on behalf of the technicians became apparent. Almost one year had been wasted on running tests which did not pay off. The first breakthrough appeared but after the involvement of the engineers at the paper factory Hahnemühle, who in conclusion of lengthy tests had identified the raw materials needed to recreate that type of paper, namely ramia fibers, a plant to be found only in South-East Asia, and first quality flax fibers.

RSHA had no other choice but import significant amounts of them from Far East and Turkey. Once having cleared that hurdle they had to face a bigger one ahead – the security features. After another year of exertions they succeeded in reproducing the watermarks and other various images incorporated into the banknotes.

Nevertheless, the operation had once been called off due to an apparent lack of results and the misunderstandings among the SS members involved, being resumed under the supervision of SS major (Sturmbannführer) Bernhard Krüger in July 1942 at the behest of Heinrich Himmler, demanding a mass production of banknotes by employing concentration camp prisoners. Taking over the work of Albert Langer, Krüger had to crack the algorithm used to generate the registration numbers and pinpoint a distinctive security mark applied on the banknotes.

In early 1943, in the Sachsenhausen concentration camp, almost thirty Jewish detainees who had previously worked in printing houses or having a similar expertise – thoroughly picked out from the extermination camps at Buchenwald, Mauthausen, Ravensbrück, Theresienstadt and Auschwitz-Birkenau – took to mass counterfeit the notes of 5, 10, 20 and 50 pounds, after the first test of the banknotes had been carried out in late 1942.

An RSHA collaborator turned up at a Swiss bank under the pretext of checking up some pounds he had acquired on the black market. After several days of careful investigations the bank experts came to the conclusion that they were real. Furthermore, they contacted the Bank of England, which admitted the banknotes were true.

From 1943 to 1945 from the printing machines at Sachsenhausen had been rolled out almost nine million banknotes at a value of almost 135 million pounds. We know this figure due to the endeavors of a detainee, Oskar Stein, tasked with registering the banknotes. Surreptitiously, he made another register where he kept an accurate count of the money, which he produced after being set free from the camp.

The banknotes counterfeited by the laborers at Sachsenhausen proved to be so well made that looked like having come out right from the Bank of England printing shop. They wanted to reach such a close similarity that a special line had been created to have the wads of banknotes clipped with safety pins the way the Brits were doing, or crinkle them up to look in use.

Despite these achievements it was apparent that in that stage of the war "Luftwaffe" could not provide the planes needed to carry out the operation, thus that other methods had been called on. Major Paul Schwend had set up a money laundering network he circulated the banknotes through, especially because the British pound was a hard currency.

They were buying from raw materials to armament in countries under their influence, or purchasing other currencies and paying spies with them, the most notorious case being that of Elyesa Bazna, the valet of the British ambassador to Ankara, who was paid 300,000 in counterfeited British pounds.

In September 1944 Major Krüger had informed the laborers they would switch to counterfeiting dollars. Avraham Sonnenfeld, whose grandparent had had a publishing house in Romania, got to Sachsenhausen right during the switching to dollar. He refers in his memoires at the renowned Salomon Smolianoff, a Russian Jew specially brought in by Krüger. Prior to the war this had been a counterfeiter sought after all over Europe, and his skills would have been put to use to carry on successfully the operation.

Despite the men the Major had got in, due to the shortage of materials until April 1945 there had been made only two hundred banknotes, but nonetheless, like the previous ones, flawless.

The closing in of the Allied armies to the Sachsenhausen camp had forced Major Krüger to disassemble the entire factory, machineries included, and ship them to another camp, the Mauthausen one, along with the laborers. The remaining counterfeited money had been put into water tight boxes and dropped into the Toplitz Lake in Austria, next to other important documents.

"Operation Bernhard" led to the production of about one sixth of the entire amount of British currency circulating in the world, more than the Bank of England's reserve. The board of the institution had to admit after the war that a significant amount of its banknotes had been counterfeited, being forced to introduce new security features. Thus, after the war, the Bank of England had to invalidate all the 5 and 10 notes as long as almost half of them were coming in fact from the Sachsenhausen camp.

The British experts could spot the forgeries but due to some intentional flaws, the Sachsenhausen banknotes being earmarked by Major Krüger into three categories relative to their quality. The first category comprised the best duplicates, but more time and labor consuming, the second category those with barely noticeable flaws, while the banknotes into the third category could be easily spotted as counterfeited at a closer look.

Finally, updated to the present value, the money counterfeited by the Jewish laborers at the Sachsenhausen camp reaches a value of over four billion Euros, while the Nazi war machine had used the equivalent of about four hundred million Euros!

THE JEWISH PRINCESS, SPY FOR NAZIS

Though of Jewish origin, Princess Stephanie Hohenlohe (1891 – 1972) had spied for Germany in USA, President Franklin D. Roosevelt himself deeming her an agent *more dangerous than one thousand men.*[LXVII]

Known also as "The spy princess of Hitler⊡s," the Jewish origin Austrian woman Stephanie had got pregnant when only 22 years old with an Archduke, the mistake being duly mended through a hasty marriage with the German Prince Friedrich Franz von Hohenlohe-Waldenburg-Schillingsfürst.

She gets a divorce in 1920 but retains her title of Princess, running riot all over Europe, embroiled in affairs with all kind of men, from British tycoons to Nazi diplomats. During that time she began being associated with Adolf Hitler, who called her "My dear princess." Stephanie was close to the Nazi elite, being thus given the title of "Honorary Arian," an unusual situation if taking into account the Nazis stance toward the Jews. In the thirties she moves to London and makes a good use of her charms to spy and go into propaganda for the Nazi cause, carrying correspondence and setting up meetings between high ranking British and Nazi officials. Thus, Stephanie managed to arrange even the controversial meeting between King Edward XVIII and his wife Wallis Simpson with the Fuhrer in 1937.

Nevertheless, like most of those knowing too much, Stephanie had been arrested by FBI and sent to Texas. She used the time she had served in prison to help OSS develop the psychological portrait of Hitler, bringing an important contribution in the making of the report "Analysis of the Personality of Adolf Hitler." After the war Stephanie had resumed her activity in Germany, looking for men to provide her a proper lifestyle.

Though of Russian origin, ballerina Malvina Lee had stolen the attack plans from the General Headquarters of the Allied forces tasked with liberating Norway invaded on April 9, 1940 by the Wehrmacht, and conveyed them later on to the Germans. Therefore it can be said without getting wrong that in the Hitler⊠s Germany the racial purity commitment had been enforced everywhere but in the espionage and the cadre policy of the Nazi leadership.

"THE FIERCE MARLENE" (DIETRICH)

Unlike those previously referred to, the persons that spied for Allies in Germany had done it out of antifascist, humanitarian convictions. Lately declassified documents have proved that diplomat Fritz Kolbe (1903 – 1971) *had been the most important spy of the Second World War,* at least for the Allies, due to the scope and importance of the documents (over 1,600) he on his own initiative had passed on to the resident of the American Office of Strategic Services (OSS) in Switzerland, Allan Dulles, regarding, inter alia, V1 and V2 rockets and other weapons, the list of the German spies in different countries, the strategic plans of Japan for South-East Asia. Despite his services on behalf of democracy *(I have been a spy with human face,* he once stated), after the war Kolbe had not been readmitted to the German Foreign Ministry, his achievements being acknowledged only in... 2004!

Actress Marlene Dietrich[227] as agent of influence, as well as the diplomat Rudolf von Schlieha (1897 – 1942) and officer Hans-Thilo Schmidt (1888 – 1943) who had conveyed important data on the German cryptographic system, paving thus the way to the breaking of the Enigma cipher machine, paying with his life for these actions, had also worked for the Allies out of sheer patriotic reasons.[LXVIII]

Coming back to the espionage activity of Marlene Dietrich, she had accepted to work for the service led by Sir William Samuel Stephenson (1897 – 1989), called on the secret front

"The Undertaker," too, the head of the British MI6 branch in USA set up to create a proper psychological climate for the US to forgo its neutrality status, with such determination that even the German secret services dubbed her "the fierce Marlene."

NETWORK TO

Even before the breaking out of the conflict with USA, Japan had stepped up its espionage activities against both that country and other states. The "network TO" consisting in Japanese diplomats accredited to neutral countries but USA also, had passed on intelligence of utmost strategic importance. Prior to the concluding of the alliance with Germany, the data gathered by "the spies under diplomatic immunity" of the Network had been conveyed to The Third Reich.

One of the most successful agents proved to be the diplomat Hiroshi Oshima who, unaware that the Japanese diplomatic code had already been "cracked" by the Americans, passed on intelligence to Germany and became unwillingly, as general George Marshall[228] pointed: *our main source of information over Hitler's intentions in Europe.*[LXIX]

OPERATION AUTONOMOUS

The attention given by both the British espionage (SOE) and the American one (OSS) to the Balkans and Romania in particular was due to its geostrategic location, resources, as well as to the eventuality of that Eastern Europe state leave the alliance with Germany.

Just in view of this latter goal, in December 1943 *the Operation Autonomous* is set off in Romania by SOE with the airdropping of John Gardyne de Chastelain, former resident in Romania of the English information service, Ivor Porter, visiting professor at the Bucharest University and officer George Silviu Mesianu. The operation aimed to make contacts with the political opposition to lay ground for the Romania getting out of the Axis ("Rome-Berlin-Tokyo Axis," an alliance between Fascist Italy, Nazi Germany and Imperial Japan to be later on joined by Finland, Hungary and Romania); establish connections with Iuliu Maniu[229] group, and mediating the talks Marshall Ion Antonescu[230] was to have to the same goal.

"Operation Autonomous" aimed likewise to intoxicate Berlin as to "Operation Bodyguard" set off to mislead the Germans over the place of the Allies landing on the continent. After getting airdropped the group involved in this mission is captured by the Romanian Gendarmerie[231]. Despite de German pressures to hand the group members over to them, these are being held in Romanian custody until August 23, 1944 when they are set free.

By the end of the war OSS resumed its activities in Romania, in particular relative to counteracting the danger of the country getting communized. In this context Charles Hostler had been dispatched to Romania in July 1945 as head of the OSS mission. He coordinates the actions meant to save persons opposing communism, seeking refuge at the US embassy, who had been later on shipped to Austria.

Frank Gardiner Wisner (1909 – 1965) was in Romania head of OSS operations in South Eastern Europe. His main assignment was to coordinate the espionage actions against the soviet troops in Romania and penetrate the Communist Party. He warns about the danger that Soviet Union take control of Eastern Europe and advises King Michael I of Romania[232] to go into exile.

After leaving Romania, Wisner is hired by CIA and joins some actions, like the plan to dig a tunnel in Berlin to spy on the soviet authorities and gaining the text of the secret report presented by General Secretary Nikita Khrushchev at the XX Congress of the Soviet Union Communist Party (1956) where the soviet leader had denounced the Stalinist purges, thus making possible a slowdown of repression in the Soviet Union.[LXX]

The British espionage did not lie idle in the Balkans, either. The famous Maria Tanase[233], "called the nightingale of the Romanian popular song," got involved in informative actions, too. There are documents over the relations between her and Eugen Cristescu[234], the head of the Romanian

Information Secret Service, whom the singer had eased an intelligence exchange with some American diplomats. Maria Tanase had been eventually arrested for having spied for the Brits, being charged of collaborating with the network headed by "Rica" Constantinescu, but the evidences against her are deemed inconclusive.

There are referred to the relations Maria Tanase would have had with a German officer, a Major from "Abwehr" who had unsuccessfully attempted to recruit her. The actress remained under surveillance after the war, too, being ascertained that she was part of the entourage of General E.R. Greer at the British Military Mission in Romania, whom she was passing on information.

"TIDAL WAVE" VS TESTER

Princess Catherine Olympia Caradja[235] acts covertly to save the American paratroopers dropped over Romania during the Second World War ("Operation Tidal Wave"), hiding them on her estate and in hospitals, reason why she was dubbed "the angel" from Ploiesti (city in Romania known as the capital of the black gold, relative to the oil fields in that region of the country). She collaborated with OSS agent Frank Wisner, but the FBI director, J. Edgar Hoover, believes she might have been a soviet spy, (too).

On the other side, the informative actions of Germany had been mostly carried out by the diplomats accredited at the mission of that country in Bucharest, due to the failure of recruiting Romanian agents. Among them are worth mentioning Karl Freiherr von Gregory, consul of the German Legation in Romania and Herr Lörner, a consul, too, proved to be information agent. The Romanian counterespionage, Siguranta[236], was closely monitoring the informative approaches of the German Legation, succeeding even in slipping an agent inside it, whose codename was "Karr."

A peculiar figure of the German espionage in Romania was Arthur Tester (1895 – 1944), actor and author. Recruited by the German intelligence services, he settles down in Great Britain, where he goes into a frantic pro-Nazi propaganda. In June 1940 he arrives to Bucharest, the capital of Romania, and carried on its anti-British propaganda. He is assigned by the German Legation the task of setting up the information service of the Romania German ethnic group branch of the German National Socialist Workers Party but in the end he got himself monitored by the German information service, being suspected of relations with the English and American services. He was involved in recruiting the agent "Doctor Ecko" (Constantine Bursan) and establishing his connections with the English espionage residence for Romania. After the coup d'état from August 23, 1944 (date when Romania got out of the alliance with Hitler and turned arms against Nazi Germany), Tester was shot to death while attempting to leave Romania. According to some authors (Jacques de Launay[237]), Tester would have been *one of the great spies of our century.*[LXXI]

THE END OF THE FIRST VOLUME...

ON THE AUTHOR

BOGDAN PAUL A. PAPADIE was born on June 13th, 1970 in Bucharest.

An active participant at the events of December 1989, standing out through the special missions he was involved in. Impressed with the bloody falling of the communist regime and the chaos reigning the Romanian society of that time he came to be one of the mass media representatives seeking frantically to reveal the truth on the new regime in charge. Though making his debut in the sport press, following in the footsteps of his father (the late well known journalist of "Gazeta Sporturilor" Aurel Papadie), later on he takes up the investigative approach, publishing in more than 25 years of journalism many press investigations and inquiries in the "Gazeta Sporturilor" (Sports Gazette), "Ora" (The Hour), "Sportul Romanesc" (The Romanian Sport), "Tineretul Liber" (The Free Youth), "Cronica Romana" (Romanian Chronicle), "Atac la Persoana" (Attack to Person), "Monitorul de Bucuresti" (The Monitor of Bucharest) publications.

He had established and ran "Ora H magazine" (H Hour Magazine), "International Jobs" and "INWA", "Inwanet Press", "Info Terra", "Bacau News" and "Terra News" press agencies.

Author and co-author of books, he took part in the making of many volumes on history and statistic of espionage, representative being "The War of Spies – Inside and Beyond the Romanian Borders", "Spies and the Revolutionary Coup", "The Brotherhood of Spies", and "Armageddon Romania."

He had studied history at the Christian University "Dimitrie Cantemir" and the ins and outs of newspaper work at "The Journalism College" – REPORTER. He is also keen on business, having graduated The Administration and Management Faculty of the "Columbia Pacific University" – Distance Learning Institutions – CPU.

In addition, he studied "OSINT – Open Source Intelligence – NATO intelligence exploitation of the Internet" (Cyber Defense Division).

He is now working on "The Brotherhood of Spies" (volumes II and III), "The Irredentist Conspiracy – Target: Romania!", and the franchise "The Spies of the Virgin Queen" (8 volumes).

EXPLANATORY NOTES
[1] (abbreviated *EU*) – An economic and political union developed in Europe, consisting of 28 states. The origins of *the European Union* are going back to the European Community of Coal and Steel (CECO) and European Economic Community (CEE) formed of six states in 1958. In the following years the European Union has expanded and increased its strength by incorporating new fields, economical, social and political, within its scope. The *Maastricht Treaty* had laid the foundations of the European Union under its present name, in 1993. The last alteration of the EU constitutional grounds had been done by the *Lisbon Treaty*, which came into force on December 1, 2009. It works through a system of supra-national and inter-governmental independent institutions which make decisions by way of negotiations between the member states. More important: *The European Union, Council of Europe, European Court of Justice and the European Central Bank.* It is governed by the European Parliament, elected every 5 years by the European citizens. The Union has developed a single market within a standardized and unified system of laws applied to all the member states. It backs and guarantees the free movement of persons, goods, services and capitals, issues laws in the fields of justice and internal affairs, preserving common policies in the fields of trade, agriculture, fishing and regional development. There had also been founded a monetary union, *Euro Zone*, comprised of 19 states. Through a *Common Policy* on foreign affairs and security EU had developed a limited role in the

international relations and security. Having a combined population of over 500 million people representing 7.3% of the world population, the European Union outputs a GDP of about 18 trillion American dollars (greater than any country's in the world) representing 20% of the assessed GDP in terms of global purchasing power parity. December 1, 2009 is the date since the European Union has an international legal personality and can sign treaties. In 2012 it had been awarded the Nobel Prize for Peace *for over six decades of contribution to the advancement of peace and reconciliation, democracy and human right in Europe.*

[2] *North Atlantic Treaty Organization* (abbreviated *NATO* in English and *OTAN* in French and Spanish, is a politically militarily alliance founded in 1949 by the North Atlantic Treaty (signed in Washington on April 4). In the present it consists of 28 states from Europe and North America. The main idea behind the alliance, held together for more than 50 years, was working out a common, credible and efficient defense against possible threats.

[3] *Sir Halford John Mackinder* (1861 – 1947), geographer, academician, English politician, the first dean of the *University Extension College* (later becoming the University of Reading – Great Britain) and dean of London School of Economics, rightly deemed one of the fathers of the global geopolitics and geostrategy.

[4] *John Forbes Kerry* (n. 1943) – Member of the United States Senate from Massachusetts. In 2004, during the

presidential campaign he ran for the Democratic Party, losing the elections to the forty third President George W. Bush. John Kerry holds the office of Secretary of State in the Barrack Obama administration from February 1, 2013.

[5] Or *Republic of Georgia*, sometimes called *Gruziya*. Country in the Caucasus region of Eurasia. It covers a territory 69,700 km^2 and has a population of 4.3 million inhabitants.

[6] Autonomous republic from Georgia which had unilaterally declared its independence in 1990. Unofficially, the independence of *South Ossetia* is backed by Russia, which had already recognized it, there being plans of uniting this territory with *North Ossetia*, an autonomous republic within Russia.

[7] Autonomous republic lying to the North West of Georgia, self-proclaimed independent, bordering the shore of Black Sea and the West of Caucasus Mountains. Created on March 4, 1921.

[8] Referring to the countries bordering the Persian Gulf (to the south *United Arab Emirates,* to the east *Saudi Arabia*, *Qatar* and *Bahrain* – an island, to the north west *Kuwait* and *Iraq* and to the north east *Iran*).

[9] Abbreviated *RM* or *R.M.* – state located in South Eastern Europe, bordering Romania to the west and Ukraine to the north, east and south. During the breakdown of Soviet Union *Moldova Republic* declared its independence on August 27,

1991. Beginning with 1990 the territory of Moldova on the eastern bank of Dniester River is under the *de facto* control of the separatist regime from Transnistria.

[10] It designates three territories: a) the *de jure* autonomous region within Moldova Republic lying to the east of Dniester (save the communes to the west of Dniester belonging to the district of Dubasari), officially called *Administrative Territorial Units to the Left of Dniester* (UATSN); b) the so called Dniester Moldova Republic (RMN), *de facto* independent self-proclaimed separatist region in control of that part of Moldova Republic to the east of Dniester (left bank) but also of six villages as well as the town of Tighina lying to the west of Dniester (therefore the *de jure* UATSN territories and RMN do not overlap exactly); c) the Ukrainian region occupied by Romania during the Second World War lying between the Bug and Dniester Rivers, including the south part of Podolia and Edisan historical region.

[11] In the Gagauzian language *Gagauz Yeri* or *Gagauziya,* the word *yeri* meaning *"land"* or *"country."* – autonomous region (from 1995) to the south west of Moldova Republic mostly inhabited by Gagauzi, people speaking a Turki language and culturally close to the Turks but of Orthodox faith. Officially the autonomous region is known as the Autonomous Territorial Unit Gagauzia (abbreviated UTA Gagauzia; in the Gaugazian language *Avtonom Territorial*

Bölümlüü Gagauziya). Its name came from the ethnonym Gagauz.

[12] The area where Danube River flows into the Black Sea, known also as *Danube Delta*. It covers 3.446 km^2 and lies mostly in Dobruja (Romania) and partly in Ukraine, the second by size and the best preserved of the Europe deltas. Since 1991 it had entered the UNESCO World Patrimony, being protected by *Ramsar Convention on Wetlands* - May 21, 1991, as internationally significant wetland.

[13] It is the expanse of water from the geo-morphological basin denominated Pontic, one of the basins in the Tethys tectonic complex, itself part of the Alpine Himalaya orogenesis, comprising also the mountains bordering it to the north (in Crimea), to the north east (Caucasus) and to the south (the Pontic ridges). It lies between Europe and Asia, having as riparian states Russia, Ukraine, Romania, Bulgaria, Turkey and Georgia. The *Black Sea* is connected, through Kerch strait, to the Azov Sea, through Bosporus to the Marmara Sea, and through Dardanelles strait to the Aegean Sea, and accordingly to the Mediterranean Sea. From a hydrological standpoint it is a remainder of the Sarmatia Sea, and displays some features to be found nowhere else in the world: low salinity waters (on average 16-18 grams salt per liter against 34-37 grams per liter in other seas and oceans), stratification between the oxygen rich shallow waters and the deep anoxic ones (phenomenon called *euxinism*), alluvium formed lakes at the river mouths,

flora and fauna comprising many relic species. On the Romanian seaside the salinity drops even lower, usually ranging between 7 and 12 per thousand. It covers 423,488 km², with the greatest depth at 2,211 meters under the sea level, close by Yalta.

[14] Historical and geographical denomination used to describe South Eastern Europe. The region covers about 55,000 km² and has a population of about 53 million people. The name of the region comes from the Balkan Mountains, which begin from the eastern Serbia and cross the center of Bulgaria. The geographers agree upon the Balkan Peninsula lying to the south of Danube River and being bounded by the Adriatic Sea, Ionian Sea, Aegean Sea and Black Sea. In accordance with this definition, the countries truly belonging to the *Balkans* are *Slovenia, Croatia, Yugoslavia* and *Albania* (with coastal borders to the Adriatic Sea), *Bulgaria* and *Turkey* (lying to the south of Danube and bounded by the Black Sea, or in case of Turkey by the Aegean Sea, too), and *Greece* (bounded by the Ionian Sea). Between these countries lies Bosnia Herzegovina. The sociologists and historians, employing more historical and social criteria, include Romania, too, in the Balkans as long as this country had been subjected to the Ottoman influence for more than five centuries.

[15] It is a village, the residence of *Deveselu* commune, Olt County, Romania. On February 4, 2010 Romania had accepted the USA proposal to locate SM-3 antimissile

ground installations at Deveselu in order to protect the south of Europe against short and intermediary range Iranian missiles. The systems are operational since 2015 and consist of three blocks of 24 SM-3 Block 1B missiles manned by about 200 American servicemen (limited at a maximum of 500). The airbase is under command of the Romanian Air Forces.

[16] Document setting forth the European Union admission calendar.

[17] *Deep and Comprehensive Free Trade Area (DCFTA)* – agreement whereby a *free trade zone* is created between the signatory state and the European Union (*ZLSAC*) providing the economic integrity of that state in EU and implying a gradual liberalization of exchanges of goods and services, free movement of the workforce, cutting down custom taxes, technical and non-tariff barriers, cancelling the quantitative restrictions and adapting the legislation of the signatory state to that of the European Union.

[18] Reunion held at the end of 2013 where the *Eastern Partnership* had to be signed. Six former soviet republics were supposed to sign it: three from Eastern Europe (*Belarus, Moldova Republic* and *Ukraine*) and three from the South of Caucasus (*Armenia, Azerbaijan* and *Georgia*). Ukraine turned down the invitation, like the guest of honor, Russia, which led to the entire reunion falling apart.

19 (*UVRBK*) – *Euro-Asian Custom Union*, or put it simpler the *Custom Union* – custom union between countries members to EurAsEc – *Russia, Belarus, Kazakhstan* – a manner of economic integration defining a unique custom area inside which the custom taxes on multilateral trade had been lifted and a new uniform taxing system of imports came into force.

[20] Known as *Crimea*, it lies on the northern shore of Black Sea. The peninsula is located to the south of Kherson region, Ukraine, and to the west is bounded by the Kuban region, Russia, being connected to Kherson through Perekop isthmus and separated from Kuban by the Kerch strait. The peninsula is surrounded by Black Sea (to the west and south) and Azov Sea (to the east).

[21] A proposal submitted to *Belarus, Kazakhstan, Kirgizstan, Russia, Tajikistan*, as well as to other states like *Finland, Hungary, Czech Republic, Bulgaria* and *Mongolia*, to strengthen the economical and political cooperation between them by way of a supranational union. On November 18, 2011 the Presidents of Belarus, Kazakhstan and Russia had signed an agreement aiming to establish the *Eurasia Union* until 2015. The agreement had comprised the roadmap delineating the future integration and set up the Eurasia Commission (by the already known model of the European Commission) and the *Eurasia Economic Region*; both would begin working on January 1, 2012.

[22] Referring to the Bosnia War, known also as the *Bosnia and Herzegovina War*, an international armed conflict that was waged between March 1992 and November 1995. Several armed units had been embroiled in the war, the conflict having interracial and religious grounds, the Bosnia Christian Serbs having fought the Muslims.

[23] Or *The Warsaw Pact*, formally named the *Treaty of Friendship, Cooperation and Mutual Assistance*, had been a military alliance of the countries from Central and Eastern Europe and the East (communist) Block wishing to defend itself against a possible NATO threat (founded in 1949). The institution of the Pact had been sped up by the integration in NATO of the remilitarized *West Germany*, furthered through the signing by the Western Countries of the *Paris Agreements*. The Warsaw Pact had been devised by Nikita Khrushchev in 1955 and signed at Warsaw in May 14, 1955. The Pact had ceased to exist on March 3, 1991, being officially dissolved at the meeting in Prague from July 1, 1991.

[24] As the Greek legend has it, the goddess Tethys, mother of the Greek hero Achilles, wishing to protect him against any possible dangers, steeped him into Styx, a river from inferno, whose water was making you invulnerable. But the goddess when steeping him into the water had held him by the heel, thus Achilles turning invulnerable save the heel Tethys had held him of. The hero had died during the Trojan War when hit by an arrow right in the heel. The expression is used to

point a vulnerable place, a weak spot of a person, but it can be used otherwise too, for instance when disclosing a flawed part of someone's line of thought – then it is said you found his *Achilles⍰ heel.*

[25] The *Marshall Plan*, officially known as *European Recovery Program* (ERP), was the first reconstruction plan devised by the United States of America and directed to the European countries affected by the Second World War. On June 5, 1947, in a speech given at the Harvard University Theatre, the American State Secretary George Marshall had made public the launching of a huge economic assistance program meant to rebuild the European economies and stem the communism, phenomenon he was seen related to economic problems. On June 19, 1947 the foreign ministers of France (Georges Bidault) and United Kingdom (Ernest Bevin) had put their signatures on a communiqué whereby they had invited 22 European states to send envoys to Paris in order to draft a plan for the European reconstruction. Labeling the "Marshall Plan" as *American economic imperialism*, Moscow forbade its satellites joining the Paris Conference. The soviets thought the plan would have led to the countries in the sphere of influence of USSR breaking away and to the losing of the political and strategic advantages Kremlin had gained in the Central and Eastern Europe at the end of the Second World War. The "Marshall Plan" does also represent the economic extension of the Truman doctrine.

[26] *Thomas Woodrow Wilson*, known mostly as *Woodrow Wilson* (1856 – 1924) had been the 28th President of the United States. A committed Presbyterian, Wilson came to be a good historian and expert in politics. During his first presidential mandate (1913 – 1917) he played a major role in setting up a system of laws to govern the *Federal Reserve System*. Reelected in 1916, he devoted himself to the participation of his country in the First World War and establishing a just peace grounded on *the right of people to dispose of themselves*, embodied in the *Fourteen points.* But these had been hotly debated at the 1919 Paris Peace Conference. Thus, the Versailles treaty with Germany, exceedingly hard in consequence of the France demands, was denying the German people *the right to dispose of itself*, out of this reason having been rejected by the US Senate. Instead, the breaking apart of the Austria-Hungary Empire had been sanctioned by the treaties at Saint-Germain and Trianon, in accordance with the 10th of the 14 points.

[27] *Sir Winston Leonard Spencer Churchill* (1874 – 1965), British politician, Prime Minister of the United Kingdom during two mandates (1940 – 1945) and (1951 – 1955). Former officer in the British Army, historian, writer and artist. The only British Prime Minister to have been awarded the Nobel Prize for Literature (1953) and the only person to be bestowed on the title of *Honorary Citizen of the United States.* Being in the forefront of the British policy for more than fifty years he held several political and ministerial offices like President of the Board of Trade, Home

Secretary, First Lord of the Admiralty, Minister of Munitions, Secretary of State for War and Secretary of State for Air, Chancellor of Exchequer (from this position he had decided in 1925 to return the pound sterling to the gold standard and creating thus a deflationary pressure on the Great Britain economy). He had fought on the Western Front, too, in the First World War as commander of the 6th battalion of the Royal Scots Fusiliers. Upon his death, by the agreement of Queen Elizabeth II, he was organized a grandiose state funeral attended by the largest number of politicians ever to congregate in history. Named the greatest Briton from all times in a 2012 opinion pool, Churchill is seen as one of the most influential persons in the history of Great Britain.

[28] Abbreviated *UN* – the most important international organization in the world. Established in 1945, after the Second World War, it has today 194 member states. Its establishment had also consisted in signing by the founding members of the *United Nations Charter*. In accordance with this document UN has the mission to *"provide global peace,"* *"observance of human rights,"* *"international cooperation"* and *"observance of the international law."* Its main headquarters is in New York.

[29] *The Bretton Woods System* of monetary management had established the norms of financial and commercial relations between the major industrialized states of the world since the middle of the XX century. *The Bretton Woods System* was

the first example of a monetary arrangement, with full negotiations, meant to regulate monetary relations between independent states. The agreement signed at Bretton Woods comprised 20 articles making up the statute of the International Monetary Fund. It was stipulated that IMF had legal personality, being a command organism with a proper budget and a procedural decision and interpretation mechanism of its own statute.

[30] *The General Agreement on Tariffs and Trade* – (abbreviated *GATT*) had been negotiated during the UN conference on Trade and Employment and resulted in consequence of the governments failure to agree upon founding the International Trade Organization (ITO). GATT had been established in 1947 and lasted until 1994 when it was superseded by the World Trade Organization (OMC) in 1995. The original provisions of GATT (GATT 1947) are still in force within OMC, subjected to the GATT alterations from 1994. In 1991 it had 104 members and special relations with other 31 states.

[31] (1886 – 1946) better known under the name *H. G. Wells*, British writer famous for his fiction books like *The Time Machine, The War of the Worlds, The Invisible Man, The First Men in the Moon and The Island of Doctor Moreau.* He had also published contemporary novels, works on history and social commentaries. He was an avowed socialist and pacifist, his works gaining later on more and more political

and didactic features. Both Wells and Jules Verne are acknowledged as *the fathers of science fiction.*

[32] *Fellowship* – fundamentalist organization of Christian roots guiding itself by the ancient writings found at the Dead Sea. The leadership structure, the manner of organization and working are unknown.

[33] *Tao Te Ching* (*Tao Te King* or *Dao De Jing*) – classical Chinese text written around 600 BC and credited to Lao Zi. It is one of the fundamental writings of Chinese philosophy for having laid the basis of Taoism.

[34] *Cecil John Rhodes* (1853 – 1902) – businessman, mining tycoon and South African politician, born and educated in Great Britain. The founder of the diamond mining and extraction company De Beers, in control today of 40% of the world raw diamonds (in the past it controlled 90% of all the diamonds extracted in the world). A staunch backer and enforcer of colonialism he had founded the state of Rhodesia (named after him, which had later separated in two states: Zambia and the actual Zimbabwe respectively). Known also for the scholarship bearing his name.

[35] (1880 – 1949) known as *Alice A. Bailey* or *AAB*, born *Alice LaTrobe Bateman.* Writer and educator. Her writings had covered many fields like: spirituality, occultism, astrology, theosophy, Christianity and other religious subjects. Her philosophy and writings are still taught in the groups and organizations she had laid foundations of, like:

Arcane School, New Group of World Servers, as well as in the meditation groups *Full Moon Meditation* following her teachings.

[36] The old and mystique order of the Rose-cross, established by Pharaoh Tutomis III – initially known as *The Great White Brotherhood.* Philosophical movement of ancient inspiration rooted in the mystery schools of the Old Egypt (the Rosicrucian temples are often decorated and erected Egyptian style to commemorate thus their traditional origins). The word mystery did not have in antiquity the meaning of today, namely that of *strange, fantastic,* designating instead a gnosis, a hidden wisdom.

[37] Abbreviation *for Readiness Exercise 1984* – a United States federal government plan aiming to test its capability to detain as many as possible American citizens in case of widespread civil unrest.

[38] Plan devised by the United States Department of Defense stipulating enforcing law and federal military assistance (National Guard intervention) for local administrations in case of serious civil unrests. The plane had been developed in response to the social movements from the sixties, now being under the control of the USA *Northern Command* (Northcom).

[39] Abbreviation of *Radio Frequency Identification.* An automatic identification system which uses electromagnetic fields to automatically identify and track tags attached to

objects by way of RFID labels and transponders. Technology requires the cooperation between a RFID reader and a RFID label.

[40] *Liz McIntyre* – Expert in the private life of the consumers who had coauthored with Katherine Albrecht the book *Spychip*: *How Major Corporations and Government Plan to Track your Every Move.* The two assert that the governments and the great corporations plan to track the move of each consumer and citizen by way of RFID, which would amount to the last step taken toward a totalitarian state surveying its citizens like in the novel 1984 penned by George Orwell.

[41] Practitioners of *Gnosticism* (from the Greek *gnōsis*, knowledge, in the Sanskrit *gnana*). Different syncretic religious movements consisting of diverse belief systems conjoined into a teaching asserting that people are divine souls locked into a material world created by a flawed God, The Demiurge, often identified with the God of Abraham.

[42] *Cabala* practitioners – an old tradition born 5770 years ago. The term Cabala comes from the Hebrew word kabbalah meaning receiving, reception. In fact the Hebrew language, seen as one of the sacred languages, had been in particular developed by and for Cabalists to help them communicate on spiritual arts. The wide access to the occult Cabala became possible only at the end of XII century through *The Book of Zohar.*

[43] (Or *Cathars*) – The Catharism is a Christian doctrine that appeared in the Middle Age. Its followers, the *Cathars* (from Greek translated as the *Pure Ones*, known also as the *Albigenses* for being especially strong in the Albi region), are a Christian sect heavily influenced by Gnosticism, whose thesis leads to extreme the doctrine of the two principles *the Good* and *the Evil*.

[44] *The Poor Fellow Soldiers of Christ and of the Temple of Solomon* (In Latin in original *Pauperes commilitones Christi Templique Solomonici*) known especially under the name *Templars*, or the *Order of the Temple* (in French in original *Ordres du Temple or Templiers*), had been one of the best known Christian (Catholic) military orders. It had been founded upon the initiative of the French Hugo de Payens in 1119, at Jerusalem, as a friar-military organization openly pledging to defend the Christian pilgrims (travelers) to the Holy Land. Officially recognized by the Catholic Church through Pope Innocent II accepting in 1139 its organizational structure, the Order grew rapidly in terms of members and power. The Order (Organization) comprised warrior friars, chaplain friars and attending friars (servants). The Templar Knights could be identified by their apparel consisting of a white mantle bearing a distinctive red cross, being among the best equipped, trained and disciplined warriors in the time of Crusades. The non warring Order members had laid foundations of a strong economic infrastructure throughout Christianity, making use for the first time of financial procedures that represented the inception of the banking

system, and erecting countless fortifications in Europe and the Holy Land (today's Israel).

The successful Templar Knights fanned up envy and the huge fortune amassed the greed of the powerful of that time. King Philip IV of France, called *the Fair*, deeply indebted to the Order began to put pressure on Pope Clement V. On November 13, 1307 King Philip had most of the Order members arrested the Grand Master Jacques de Molay included, and after getting their confessions under torture had burned them at the stake. In 1312 Pope Clement, constrained by King Philip, had forcefully dissolved the entire Order.

[45] see [36]

[46] An important token of *The Supreme Being,* borrowed by Masons from the ancient religions, *the All-seeing Eye* (*the Eye of God*) or *the Providence Eye*, graphically represented as an eye surrounded by rays, usually within a triangle.

[47] *National Mall and Memorial Parks*, national park in downtown Washington, District of Columbia, the capital of the United States of America, seen as a symbol of American democracy values. Here are famous monuments like *Washington Monument, Lincoln Memorial, World War II Memorial, Thomas Jefferson Memorial, Vietnam Veterans Memorial, Martin Luther King Jr. Memorial, Franklin Delano Roosevelt Memorial,* as well as others dedicated to

important names in the American history. *National Mall and Memorial Parks* is visited yearly by about 24 million people.

[48] Building in downtown Winnipeg (Canada) initially called *Manitoba Parliamentary Building*. Erected in a neoclassical style, it was completed in 1920 and stands 253 feet tall. It was designed and built by Frank Worthington Simon and Henry Boddington III along with other masons. The building is renowned for the *Golden Boy*, a gilded bronze statue representing the Roman god Mercury (the equivalent of the Greek god Hermes).

[49] Deemed as a Masonic landmark, *Denver International Airport* (IATA: DEN, ICAO: KDEN, FAA LID: DEN), covering 140 km², is by surface the largest international airport in the United States and second in the world to King Khalid Airport in Saudi Arabia. Runway *16R/34L* is the longest runway open to the public in the United States.

[50] *High Frequency Active Auroral Research Program* – Research program on active auroral frequencies carried out over the territory of the United States nearby Gakona, Alaska. It is a study both on ionosphere, nitrogen and their ions related to the solar and cosmic radiation bombardment and high (HF) or low frequency (LF) radiation emission from Earth. Being a scientific program the American government earmarks annually an official budget of 30 million dollars. HAARP is carried out by the *Geophysical Institute of the Alaska University* (Fairbanks) for the *Department of Defense*, *Us Navy* and *US Air Force*

respectively. HAARP is linked to one of the most powerful computers in the world of type CRAY-YMP/TM3D/T3E, the system itself being located on a military base nearby Gakona, Alaska, beneficiary of this project being *US Space Force*. Project HARP consists of ground equipment made up from a network of antennas, each antenna being supplied by its own generator and able to warm regions of ionosphere through radio waves. As of today there have been built 48 antennas, in the end being envisaged the building of up to 360 antennas. American publications *Fairbanks Daily News* and *Cooper River Country Journal* had run in September 1995 articles claiming that project HAARP would have concealed objectives, more precisely it representing an ultimate weapon with outstanding performances revolutionizing warfare entirely, being the first weapon system of universal and cosmic value.

[51] *SSSS*, sometimes called *S-quad* or *Squad* (quadrate) – Human mind alteration mechanism based on the subliminal carrier technology. It had been developed by Dr. Oliver Lowery from Norcross, Georgia (USA) and set forth in the US Patent No. 5159703, titled Silent Subliminal Presentation System, from October 27, 1992.

[52] Operation based on subliminal coordination of *Manchurian Candidate* type.

[53] It is an umbrella term for a series of experiments and programs launched by the American governments aiming directly to improve particular identification and training

methods of the so called Psy agents – future paranormal agents gathering critical data for the American Army and intelligence agencies of Washington.

[54] *Benedict XVI*, in Latin *Benedictus PP. XVI*, born Joseph Alois Ratzinger (1927), former Pope of the Catholic Church, elected (April 19, 2005) as successor of Pope John Paul II. At the same time he held the office of bishop of Rome and sovereign of the Vatican state. He is the 265th pope in the history of the Roman Catholic Church and the first German pope after 482 years (the last German pope was Pope Adrian VI between 1522 and 1523). Prior to his election as pope cardinal Ratzinger was dean of the cardinals college, prefect of the Congregation for the Doctrine of Faith and president of the International theological pontifical commission. After making public his retreat on February 11, 2013 he forwent the office on February 28, 2013. His new title is that of *pope emeritus*.

[55] In Latin *(Praelatura Sanctae Crucis et Opus Dei, The Work of God)* – Institution of the Catholic Church, a personal prelacy aiming to contribute to the spread of Gospel through church and disseminate the universal calling to holiness in the daily life. Personal prelacies are hierarchical values of the Catholic Church consisting of laymen and priests under the guidance of a prelate. *Opus Dei* had been founded by Pope John Paul II as personal prelacy through the Apostolic Constitution *Ut sit*, on November 28, 1982. The Pope had promulgated the regulations of *Opus Dei*

prelacy representing its particular law. It was firstly founded by Josemaría Escrivá de Balaguer (1902 – 1975), at Madrid on October 2, 1928. In accordance with the *Pontifical Directory*, as of today there are 90,000 persons all over the world on the prelacy. Its headquarters, along with the prelacy church, is in Rome.

[56] Bank of Vatican opened in Rome (1606). It had been working under this name until 1992.

[57] (1552 – 1621) born bearing the name *Camillo Borghese*, he had been pope from May 16, 1605 until death.

[58] *Michael Barkum* (born 1938) – Professor emeritus of politics at the *Maxwell School of Citizenship and Public Affairs*, Syracuse University, specialized in the extremism policy and relation between religion and violence. He has authored several books on this field.

[59] In Chinese pinyin, *sūn zǐ bīng fǎ*) – book written by Chinese general Sun Tzu in the VI century BC, addressing military tactics and strategies. The Art of War, consequential work of Chinese military strategy comprising 395 fight tactics recommendations (as verses), includes 13 chapters: *Laying Plans*, *Waging War*, *Attack by Stratagem*, *Tactical Dispositions*, *Energy*, *Weak Points and Strong*, *Maneuvering*, *Variation in Tactics*, *The Army on the March*, *Terrain*, *The Nine Situations*, *The Attack by Fire* and *The Use of Spies*.

It is the gist of psychological war (to have the adversary believe it is in a weak position or got to surrender) employed especially in the Vietnam or Indochina War (decades 4-5 of the XX century).

[60] *Sun Tzu Wu Chi Lieh Chuan*, in brief *Sun Tzu*, pronounced Sūn Zĭ - in pinyin, (about 544 – 496 BC) – Chinese general from the Chinese province Ch'i, the author of the textbook *The Thirteen Commandments* (known also *as The Art of War*).

[61] In the Paran Wilderness – from Madian land or Wadi Feiran of the present, where we find the ancient Refidim now bearing the name Feiran, often called *The Pearl of Sinai.*

[62] *Jericho* – (Standard: *Yəriḥo*; Canaan: *Yareah*; in Hebrew: *moon*) – town in Palestine on the east bank of Jordan. The capital of Jericho region with a population of 20,416 Palestinians (2016). It lies to the north of the *Judean Desert*, about 7 km off the Jordan River, 12 km northwest from the *Dead Sea* and 30 km northeast off Jerusalem. It is deemed the oldest settlement as well as the first fortified community in the world, many times referred to in the Holy Bible under the name the City of Palms. It has been inhabited from about 9,000 BC.

[63] (1303 – 1213), known as *Ramses the Great*; Ozymandias – in the Greek language.

[64] (1274 BC) – the coronation of Ramses II had taken place at the *Shemu* festival – May 31, 1279 BC.

[65] or *Khsayares*, the son of Darius the Great, absolute ruler of the Persian Empire between 486 – 465 BC.

[66] Inhabitants of the state city *Sparta* in the ancient Greece from the Peloponnese peninsula, on Eurotas River. Renowned for the austere life they led and their hard military training. They stood out as elite warriors.

[67] Former King in Sparta between 489/488 and 480 BC.

[68] In Greek *Megas Alexandros* (356 – 323 BC) – his spectacular conquests made the Macedonians the rulers of Middle East. On his death, aged 32, Alexander was the master of the greatest empire ever conquered. *Alexander the Great* had contributed much to the spread of the Hellenistic culture all over the world.

[69] Known also as *Darius I the Great* or *Diryayas*, the son of Hystaspes and father of Xerxes I, king of the Persians between 522 – 486 BC.

[70] Legendary poet and raphsode credited with the writing of Iliad and Odyssey. In antiquity he was credited the entire *Epic Cycle* comprising other poems, too, about the *Trojan War*, as well as Theban poems on Oedipus and his sons. Other works, like *Homeric Religious Songs,* comical mini-epopee *Batrachomyomachia* (*The War between Frogs and*

Mice) and Margites epopee had been attributed to him but as of today these facts are regarded as unreliable.

[71] Or *Iliad*, is an epopee credited to Homer, who seemed to be an aoidos from Ionia, from the second half of the VIII century BC, who had accommodated in his epopees Iliad and Odyssey traditions, fragments and motifs from old myths and popular songs. Iliad consists of 15,337 dactylic hexameters, since Hellenistic era being divided into 24 chants. The text had been composed between 850 and 740 BC (dates already referred to by Herodotus), therefore four centuries after the time the historians set the mythical war it depicts.

[72] The son of Nauplius – King of Euboea – and Clymene, hero of the *Trojan War*.

[73] Or *Odysseus* – mythological character, famous Greek hero and King of Ithaca.

[74] The youngest son of Laomedon, father of Paris and Hector.

[75] Daughter of Zeus and Metis, identified by the Romans with Minerva.

[76] (59 – 17 BC) – Roman historian, author of a monumental history of Rome, *Ab urbe condita* (also abbreviated *a.U.c.* or *AUC* – title possible inspired from the famous Latin expression meaning *since the founding of the City*, namely of Rome, used by the Roman ancient historians to date events

through referring to the legendary date of founding of Rome by *Romulus* – year 753 a.U.c. is considered year 1 of the Christian era), penned between 27 – 25 BC.

[77] Known also as *Philip II* (382 – 336 BC) – King of Macedonia between 359 – 336 BC and father of Alexander the Great.

[78] (247 – 183 BC) – Carthaginian politician and general deemed as one the most brilliant military commanders in history and one of the greatest enemies of Rome.

[79] *Polybios* or *Polybius* (about 201 – about 120 BC) son of Lycortas – Greek politician and historian native of Megalopolis locality, author of an ample history of the Mediterranean world – between 218 BC (breaking out of the second Punic war) and 146 (conquering and destruction of Cartagena).

[80] *Publius Cornelius Scipio Africanus*, known as *Scipio the African* (235 – 183 BC) – Roman general and politician, strategist during the Punic Wars.

[81] Took place around October 19, 202 BC.

[82] King of Numidia – late III century BC.

[83] *Hannon the Great* (3rd century BC) – Carthaginian general and politician, representative of the local oligarchy and leader of the pro-Roman party in Cartagena. Avowed adversary of Hamilcar Barca and Hannibal.

[84] *Publius Ventidius Bassus* - *Publius Ventidius Publii filius Bassus*, "Publius Ventidius, the son Publius, the son of Bassus" (in Latin: *P · VENTIDIVS · P · F · BASSVS*) – Roman general and one of the clients of Julius Caesar. Had won impressive victories against the Parthians that led to the death of their most important leaders. His successes made up entirely for the losses experienced by Crassus (Marcus Licinius Crassus Dives – 115/114 – 53 BC, politician in the time of the Roman republic renowned for his fortune) and paved the way for the great victories of Marc Antonius (Marcus Antonius – 82 – 30 BC). According to Plutarch, in *The Life of Antonius*, those three great military victories against the Parthians despite going down in history had not been appropriately recognized (prior to Plutarch having written about them – author's note), the Roman general having not been organized a triumphal parade as usual in that time.

[85] (238 BC – 226 BC) – the third Persian Empire that ruled over the present day Iranian plateau. Led by the Arsacid dynasty, at the height of its power was ruling over present day territories from Armenia, Mesopotamia, Iran and Afghanistan.

[86] *Titus Flavius Domitianus* (51 – 96 AD) – Roman emperor from the famous Flavian dynasty, from 81 to 96 AD.

[87] *Publius Aelius Traianus Hadrianus* (76 – 138 AD) – Roman emperor (117 – 138 AD). Hadrian was the third of the so called *the five good emperors of the Roman Empire.*

[88] *Augustus Octavian Caesar* (63 BC – 14 AD).

[89] *Gaius Aurelius Valerius Diocletianus* (244 – 311 AD) – emperor of Rome between November 20, 284 and May 1, 305.

[90] *Mithridates, Mithradates VI Eupator* – Hellenistic king of the Pontus (112 – 63 BC). One of the great intellectuals of that time and the last outstanding politician of the Hellenistic world. He accedes to power through a palace coup killing his mother and brother in the wake of it and sets up an authoritarian regime. Afraid of reprisals he got himself immune to poison. Fierce adversary of Rome he waged three wars against the Romans, extending his authority over the north and west shores of the Black Sea. Many Greek cities, among which *Tyras, Histria, Tomis* and *Callatis* acknowledged his sovereignty, being included in the *Mithridates Alliance* (I century BC). After the third war against the Romans (74 – 63 BC) Mithridates had lost the territories he had conquered and committed suicide.

[91] *Marius Caius* (about 157 – 86 BC) – Roman general and politician. He carried out an important military reform and set up an army consisting of professional soldiers. In Africa he had defeated Iugurta (King of Numidia), and both the Tetons and Cimbri (102 and 101 BC) on several battles fought in the Northern Italian Peninsula. During the Roman civil War he became the leader of Populares vying for power with the Optimates (aristocrats) headed by Sulla.

[92] Roman general and dictator (137 – 78 BC) the vanquisher of Mithridates, the head of the aristocratic party, adversary of Marius, renowned for his cruelty and sending people to death outside law.

[93] *Caesar* (100 – 44 BC) – Roman politician, general, writer and rhetorician. One of the greatest strategists of antiquity. He had concluded in 60 BC along with Crassus and Pompeii the political alliance known as *triumvirate*. Consul in 60 BC he became governor of *Gallia Narbonensis* province (58 BC) and led brilliantly the conquest campaign of the whole *Gallia* (58 – 51 BC) which he had transformed into a Roman province. By crossing the *Rubicon* he started the civil war (49 BC), defeated Pompeii at Pharsalos (48 BC) and his confederates at Thapsus (46 BC) and Munda (45 BC), practically instituting his own dictatorship. In 45 BC he had introduced the Julian calendar. He was killed at the Ides of March (March 15, 44 BC) in Senate by a conjuration Crassus and Brutus had been leading. Gifted rhetorician and writer, Caesar had authored the works *Comentarii de Bello Gallico* and *Comentarii de Bello civili*.

[94] *Gnaeus Pompeius Magnus* or *Cnaeus Pompeius Magnus* (106 – 48 BC) – Roman general and politician, one of the most famous statesmen of antiquity. Son of *Gnaeus Pompeius Strabo*, representative of a senatorial family, Pompeii gets to the forefront of political life after the landing of Sulla in the south of Italy and the breaking out of a new civil war between Populares and Optimates. In early 83 BC

he recruits 3 legions with which he makes his contribution to the victory of the Optimates (the Roman aristocracy party). In Italy (71 BC) he conquers the last remnants of the Spartacus army, one year later being elected consul along with Crassus. In 66 BC, despite the Senate opposition, he was assigned supreme command in the East during the war against Mithridates VI, the King of Pontus, whom he defeats. In 60 BC takes shape the first triumvirate between Pompeii, Caesar and Crassus, private and secrete agreement of the three of them against senatorial aristocracy. The death of Crassus at Carrhae and the glory of Caesar in Gallia led to the unraveling of the *triumvirate* and the Pompeii's approach to Senate. In 52 BC the Senate agrees upon appointing Pompeii consul sine collega, tasked with restoring order. On January 7, 49 BC, through a *senates consultum ultimum*, Caesar is removed from his positions and Pompeii commissioned to defend the Republic. Three days later, when crossing the *Rubicon* with his legions, Caesar unleashes the civil war by saying the famous words *Alea iacta est* ("the die is cast" – according to the chronicle of Suetonius). Pompeii seeks refuge in Greece where he defeats Caesar in the Battle at Dyrachium, but is vanquished (August 9, 48 BC) in the Battle at Pharsalus, Thessaly, though outnumbering Caesar two times. Defeated, Pompeii seeks refuge to Egypt where is assassinated (September 28, 48 BC) upon the order of King Ptolemy XIII (Theos Philopator).

[95] (About 46 – 125 AD) – In Greek *Ploutarkhos*, he adopted the name *Mestrius Plutarchus* – writer and moralist of Greek origin mostly known through his biographical and philosophical works. He was one of the main representatives of Atticism in the Greek literature.

[96] (55/60 – 106 AD), known also as *Decebalus per Scorilo* ("Decebal, the Son of Scorilo") – King of Dacia (87 – 106). Dacia was at the height of its power under the reign of King Decebal, the state being strong and well organized. Then the Dacian society made important headways on many fields: a large population centered around numerous davas (fortified settlements) throbbing with economic activity, having established trade routes in the Greek-Roman world, and defined by a flourishing culture bearing manifold original traits. The riches of the state led by Decebal had aroused the interest of Rome, which conquers Dacia in 106 AD after two bloody wars 101 – 102 and 105 – 106, though initially the Dacians had won the battle at Tapae (where they had wiped out Legion V). Worth noticing, by way of the mythical treasure of the Dacian Kingdom and the gold mined from Rosia Montana, the Roman Empire would recover financially and avoid an economic collapse, pushing through several centuries more.

[97] A country inhabited in antiquity by *Getae* and *Dacians*, covering territories from today's Romania, Moldova Republic, Ukraine and Hungary. Getae and Dacians were divided into a greater number of states sweeping over a

territory bounded by: Tisza River (west), Dniester River and Black Sea (east), Danube (south) and the Forested Carpathian Mountains (north). Greeks call the *Dacians Getae*, and the *Romans Dacians*. The *Dacian Kingdom* had reached its greatest expansion during the reign of *King Burebista* (King of Getae Dacians between 84 - 44 BC), being bounded by: the Black Sea shore and Bug River – to the east, Bohemian quadrate, Pannonia Danube and Morava – to the west, Forested Carpathian Mountains – to the north, and Mount Haemus (Balkan Ridge) – to the south. The capital of the kingdom was Argedava (now Popesti, Giurgiu County – Romania).

[98] *Lucius Claudius Cassius Dio* (155 or 163/164 – about 229), called also *Dio Cassius, Cassius Dio* or *Cassius Dio Cocceianus* – well known historian from the Roman empire. He had published a history of Rome (*Romaika*) in Greek, comprising 80 volumes, beginning with the arrival of Aeneas in Italy, the founding of the city and going up to the year 229, spanning thus a period of 983 years. Of the 80 volumes written over 22 years most of them made it to us in the original form or by fragments.

[99] *Justinian I*, called the *Great (Flavius Petrus Sabbatius Justinianus)* – Byzantine emperor (The Eastern Roman Empire) - between 527 – 565 AD.

[100] Or *Theodora* (about 500 – 548 AD) – she went down in history as one of the most important Byzantine empresses. She was the wife of Justinian I, being canonized and

celebrated by the Orthodox Church each year on November 14.

[101] The *Nika* riots from Constantinople. The antagonists of Justinian had proclaimed another emperor, Hepatius, the nephew of the former emperor Anastasius I. While Justinian believed everything was lost, Empress Theodora stood against withdrawal from the capital. Through talks Narses carried out with the rebels and the surprise attack conducted by Belisarius ahead of the troops loyal to the Emperor in the hippodrome, where the rebels had gathered, the revolt had been crushed.

[102] *The Eastern Roman Empire*, *Byzantine Empire* or *Byzantium* are terms conventionally used nowadays to designate the Roman Empire of Middle Age with the capital at Constantinople (today Istanbul). The official name was *Romania* or *Basileia Romaion*, *Roman Empire*. The change occurring during the reign of Heraclius I (Heraclius had Hellenized the empire about 640 by adopting Greek as official language) is seen as the discontinuation with the Roman past of Byzantium, and re-designation afterwards of the empire as *Byzantium* instead of *Eastern Roman.* But nevertheless most of the population in the European region of the Empire, save the Greeks, had carried on talking Latin vulgate until de apparition of the migrant people languages (Slavs and Bulgarians).

[103] *Renaissance* had been a cultural movement spanning XIV and XVII centuries. It firstly appeared in Italy during the

Middle Age to spread later on to the rest of Europe. Though the invention of the printing machine had sped up dissemination of ideas in the XV century, the changes brought by *Renaissance* had not been uniformly experimented throughout Europe.

[104] (1457 – 1509) – King of England (1485 – 1509). He is unanimously deemed the founder of the *House of Tudor* and that who brought to an end the *Wars of the Roses* by marrying Elizabeth of York, the daughter of Edward IV. He had disbanded the seigniorial troops and established the *Star Chamber*.

[105] (1473 – 1530) – Catholic Cardinal (1514 – 1529) in office also as Lord Chancellor and practically in control on behalf of king of the domestic and foreign policy. Henry VIII, in love with Anne Boleyn, wished to marry her with a view of having a legitimate heir, but as long as then there was no institution of divorce he had to ask the Pope to annul the marriage. Wolsey was in charge of the talks with Rome, but Charles Quint, the nephew of the Queen, stood against the divorce. Pope Clement dispatches Cardinal Campeggio to England to assess the case along with *Wolsey*, but the Queen succeeds in having the case going to trial in Rome. Sure about him being the traitor, Anne Boleyn pressed on and had her way by *Wolsey* being removed from all his official positions in 1529. The Cardinal set about at once to mastermind a public plot aiming to force Anne Boleyn going into exile and began talks with Queen Catherine and the

Pope in Rome to this end. When news on the plot transpired Henry ordered that Wolsey was arrested and without him dying due to the illness he was suffering of (1530) he would have been put to death for treason.

[106] *The First Earl of Essex* (1485 – 1540) – English lawyer and statesman who served as chief minister to King Henry VIII of England from 1532 to 1540. Cromwell was one of the strongest and most powerful advocates of the English Reformation. He helped to engineer an annulment of the king's marriage to Queen Catherine of Aragon so that Henry could lawfully marry Anne Boleyn. Later on Cromwell had reformed the Church of England, being appointed viceregent and vicar-general. During his rise to power Cromwell made many enemies, including his former ally Anne Boleyn on which downfall he played an important role. Later on, after arranging the king's marriage with Anne de Cleves he fell from power, is accused of infamy and executed for treason and heresy in Tower Hill on July 28, 1540.

[107] (1491 – 1547) – King of England from April 21, 1509 until his death. He was the second monarch of the House of Tudor, succeeding to his father. Though the second son of Henry VII and Elizabeth of York, as his older brother, Arthur, *Prince of Wales,* had died in 1502 leaving him heir to the throne, *Henry VIII* was the following sovereign of the *House of Tudor*. He is famous for having had no less than six wives: *Catherine de Aragon*, *Anne Boleyn*, *Jane Seymour*, *Anne de Cleves*, *Catherine Howard* and *Catherine Parr*.

[108] *Christopher Kit Marlowe* (1564 – 1593) – English playwright, poet and translator of the Elizabethan era. The foremost Elizabethan tragedian of his day, before Shakespeare, Kit Marlowe is known for the use of blank verse and his characters overreaching the public, as well as for his own death.

[109] (1533 – 1603) - Queen of England and Ireland from November 17, 1558 until her death. She was the daughter of Henry VIII and Anne Boleyn, executed less than three years after Elizabeth□s birth. Elizabeth I was the fifth and last monarch of the House of Tudor (Henry VII, Henry VIII, her stepbrother Eduard VI, her cousin Jane Grey and her stepsister, Mary I). Her stepbrother Edward had reigned until his death in 1553, when he left as heiress to the throne *Lady Jane Grey*, breaching thus the *Succession to the Crown Act* of Henry VIII. But the will of Edward is dismissed, Jane Grey is executed and followed by Mary I, the stepsister of Elizabeth. Five years later Elizabeth became queen at the age of twenty five and swears to care for (*England, author□s note*) until death. Because despite many proposals she had never married the House of Tudor became extinct on her death. She was also known as *The Virgin Queen*, *Gloriana* and *Good Queen Bess*. She surrounded herself with a group of trustful counselors led by William Cecil, 1st Baron Burghley. In politics she proved more moderate than her father, brother and sister. One of her mottoes was *video et taceo* ("I see and say nothing"). She engaged into a cautious diplomacy with respect to the great powers of that time,

France and Spain. After the breaking out of the England Spain War the latter had attempted to conquer England, the defeat of the Armada (the *Invincible Armada*) being one of the greatest victories in the history of England. The entire reign of Queen Elizabeth I is called *The Elizabethan Era* or the *golden age*, being defined by an increase of the England's power in the world. It was also a period of extraordinary artistic and cultural efflorescence: playwrights William Shakespeare, Christopher Marlowe and Ben Jonson being only some of the literates that had lived during her reign. Like her father, King Henry VIII, Elizabeth wrote poetry and prose. In that period Francis Drake became the first seafarer to have circled the globe; Francis Bacon set forth his political and philosophical visions and proposed the settling of North America under Sir Walter Raleigh and Sir Humphrey Gilbert. Her reign had also been defined by caution as to bestowing honors and dignities. During the tenure of Queen *Elizabeth I* but eight people had been ascended to nobility: one earl and seven barons! *Elizabeth I* had also cut down the number of her privy counselors from thirty nine to nineteen and later on to fourteen.

[110] (1552 – 1605) – member of the English Parliament, courtier and diplomat in France during the reign of Queen Elizabeth I. He was embroiled in the talks for a proposed marriage between Elizabeth I and Francis, *Duke of Anjou*. After being appointed in 1583 ambassador to Paris he took money from Henri I, *Duke of Guise*, in exchange for providing him access to his diplomatic correspondence. He

had also taken money from a Spanish agent, Bernardino de Mendoza, and there is strong evidence which convinced many historians that *Stafford* had sent secrets to Spain in exchange of money. Moreover, it was his duty to report to London any intelligence on the forming of the *Spanish Armada* but he failed in that. The head of the Elizabethan espionage, Francis Walsingham, was utterly convinced by the betrayal of *Stafford* but he was unable to act and prove anything as long as *Stafford* wad under the protection of *Lord Burghley*. Out of state reasons no actions had been taken against him by Elizabeth I after he retired from diplomacy in 1590.

[111] Head of the *Royal Council*, of the secret services of Elizabeth I of England and the longest running regal lover. He commanded the secret world of that time, being a promoter of the full aristocratic espionage with consequences borne throughout society. He laid foundations of one of the best secret services in history, its achievements taking England during the following centuries to the status of first (colonial) power of the world.

[112] Known in the English literature under the name *Mary I of Scotland* or *Mary, Queen of Scots* (1542 – 1587) she became Queen of Scotland in 1542 when only one week old! Mary was beheaded in the London Tower, being charged with conspiracy and treason against her cousin Queen Elizabeth I of England. Due to the charges, the trial and her

condemnation she ended up being known as the monarch who met one of the most distressing fates in history.

[113] (Known as *Felipe II de Habsburgo* – Spanish or *Filipe I* – Portuguese; 1527 – 1589) – King of Spain between 1556 and 1598, King of Naples and Sicily (1554 and 1589), King of England and Ireland (coregent with Mary I) between 1554 and 1558, King of Portugal and Algarve (as Philip I, 1580 – 1598) and King of the General Capitanate of Chile (Kingdom of Chile, 1554 – 1556), He was authoritarian sovereign prince of *The Seventeen Provinces* from 1556 until 1581, having many titles of duke or count for given territories. Known as *Philip the Prudent*, he ruled over one of the greatest empires in history comprising regions on all the continents then known by the Europeans. During his reign Spain was the greatest power in the Western Europe and reached its outermost influence and supremacy, undertaking explorations all over the world and settling territories on all the discovered continents. Philippines Islands had been named after him.

[114] *Henry I, Prince of Joinville, Duke of Guise, Count of Eu* (1550 – 1588) – French nobleman, member of a branch of the House of Lorena. On December 22, 1588 Henry I spent the night with his mistress, Charlotte de Sauve, notorious member of the women spy group of Catherine de' Medici. On the following morning, at Blois Castle, de Guise had been assassinated by the king's guardsman while Henry III was looking on. The brother of de Guise, Cardinal Louis

II had also been assassinated on the following day. The deeds had aroused the anger of their next of kin, and Henry III was compelled to seek refuge at *Henry de Navarra*. The king had been assassinated the following year by Jacques Clément, an agent of the Catholic League of the *House of Guise*.

[115] (1564 – 1616) – English playwright and poet regarded as the greatest writer in the English literature. He is often called *England's national poet* and the *Bard of Avon* or the *Swan of Avon*. His works, some collaborations included, consisting of approximately 38 plays, 154 sonnets, two long narrative poems, and a few other verses, have outlived him. His plays have been translated into every major living language and are performed more often than those of any other playwright. Many of his plays had been performed at the Globe Theatre, one of the most popular in the Elizabethan era, whose motto was *Totus mundus agit histrionem*, reprised in *As you Like it* in the form of the world seen as a theatre stage: *All the world's a stage, And all the men and women merely players*: *They have their exits and their entrances.* The most important rival of Shakespeare's in that time was another great playwright, Christopher Marlowe.

[116] *Anthony Babington* (1561 – 1586) – English conspirator and fanatical Catholic who led the Babington Conspiracy, backed by the catholic forces of the Middle Age Europe. While the Scottish Queen Mary I Stuart was detained at *Fotheringay Castle*, Babington along with the detainee and

other conspirators had planned to assassinate the Queen of England, Elizabeth I. Followed and exposed by the secret services faithful to the English monarchy, Anthony Babington had been arrested in 1586, charged with treason and executed.

[117] It is related to the name of Richard Chancellor, who sailed the White Sea in 1553 and resumed later on his travel on ground up to Moscow. Upon returning to England he had founded *English Muscovy Company* along with Sebastian Cabot, Sir Hugh Willoughby and several other rich London merchants. Tsar *Ivan the Terrible* had used these merchants to exchange correspondence with Queen Elizabeth I of England, being also possible to have asked through it her hand.

[118] Geographic area of the globe comprising North America, South America, Oceania, and the Australia continent. This term has been in use since XVI century and referring to the territories discovered beyond the Atlantic Ocean (*America*). Virtually, the denomination had been ascribed in opposition to the *Old World* including Europe, Asia and Africa.

[119] (About 1540 – 1596) – freebooter, seafarer, slave trader and English politician from the Elizabethan era. He was the second commander of the British fleet that fought the Spanish armada in 1588. It was the first Englishman to have circumnavigated the globe, from 1577 to 1580, and upon his return he was knighted by Queen Elizabeth I of England. He died of dysentery after having unsuccessfully attacked San

Juan (Puerto Rico) in 1596. His deeds almost made the stuff of legends and turned him into a hero for the English people while for the Spaniards he was an embodiment of the devil. *Drake* had been known as *El Draque* ("The Dragon"), the literary translation of his name, in consequence of his actions. King Philip II had put a bounty of 20,000 ducats (about 10 million dollars in today⬚s exchange rates) on his head. While in England he was mourned the Spaniards were feting.

[120] (In Spanish *Armada Invencible*) – the name of the fleet deployed in 1588 by the King of Spain Philip II to convey and support the landing of the Spanish army in England. The ensuing naval battle was part of a larger conflict between Spain and England aiming both to exploit the riches of the *New World.*

[121] *Alessandro Farnese*, Spanish *Alejandro Farnesio* (1545 – 1592) – *Duke of Parma and Piacenza* from 1586 until 1592 and Governor of the Habsburg Low Countries from 1578 until 1592. It is known for the successful campaign from 1578 – 1592 directed against the Dutch Revolt, where he had conquered the main southern cities (Belgium of today) and gave them back to the Catholic Spain.

[122] *Armand-Jean I. du Plessis de Richelieu*, went down in history as *Cardinal Richelieu*, (1585 – 1642) – former clergyman, French nobleman and politician. He had the titles *Marquis du Chillou, Bishop of Luçon* (1608), *cardinal* (1622), *prime-duke de Richelieu* (1631) and *prime-duke of*

Fronsac (1634), *Abbot of Cluny, Cîteaux* and *Prémontré*. Also called the Red Eminence, was the closest counselor of Louis XIII, his goal being the transforming of the French state structure into an absolute monarchy and weakening the Habsburg hegemony in Europe.

[123] *Alexandre Dumas - Dumas Davy de la Pailleterie*, known as *Alexandre Dumas-père* (1802 – 1870) – author of adventure and period novels whereby he became the most popular French writer in the world.

[124] Born *Giulio Raimondo Mazzarino* (1602 – 1661) – Italian cardinal, diplomat and politician, Prime Minister of France from 1642 until his death. Mazarin succeeded to his mentor, *Cardinal Richelieu*. A collector of art and jewels (especially diamonds) which he bequeathed to King Louis XIV; some of them remained in the collection at the *Louvre Museum*. The books Mazarin collected formed the basis of the *Mazarin Library* in Paris.

[125] Or *Ferdinand of Bavaria,* in German *Ferdinand von Bayern* (1577 – 1650). He was recognized as Prince-elector, Archbishop of the Archdiocese of Cologne (*Roman Holy Empire*), 1612 – 1650, and successor of Ernst of Bavaria. He was likewise Prince-bishop of Hildesheim, Liege, Munster and Paderborn.

[126] (1548 – 1600) – Renaissance Italian theologian and humanist philosopher. Condemned and burned at the stake by Inquisition for his pantheistic belief and conviction about

the plurality of the worlds, ideas deemed as heretical. His name became equivalent to that of a victim of obscurantism.

[127] (1577 – 1640) – the most renowned Flemish painter. The life of *Rubens* looks like having been ruled by a boundless energy. Within 40 years the artist had been executing 1,400 paintings and hundreds of drawings. He is warmly welcomed both into the circles of the most famous artists of that time in Europe and the princely courts.

[128] Or *Romanian Principalities* – voivodeships inhabited mostly by Romanian speaking people. They had formed in the Middle Age over the Carpathian Danube territory, vernacularly designated as the Romanian Provinces: Transylvania, Moldova, Wallachia and Dobruja.

[129] (Likewise called in the medieval documents *Ivanco Basarab, Bassarada* or *Bazarad*) dubbed in the present time Basarab the Founder (1310 – 1352) – regarded as the founder of Wallachia. He was the son of Tihomir or Thocomerius, according to an official document issued in 1332 by the King of Hungary Carol Robert d'Anjou who, after the Battle of Posada from November 1330 was rewarding the County Leader *Laurentius of Zarand* for the bravery shown in battle. The content of that diploma comprises also the mention *Basarab, filium Thocomerii, scismaticum, infidelis Olahus Nostris*.

[130] (1355 – 1418) – Voivode and Prince (leader, king) of Wallachia (1386 – 1394 and 1397 – 1418). In the official

documents he is referred to as *In the Godly Christ and Christ loving and the sole prince, I Mircea great Voivode and Prince.* In the Romanian historiography he is also mentioned under the name *Mircea the Great.* During the reign of Mircea the Elder Wallachia had reached its largest territorial expansion. This led to a strengthening of his authority expressed in the title (comprising the name Despot of the Dobrotici⯑ provinces – Dobruja and the Quadrate, regions from the present Romania and Bulgaria), and in the numismatic representations.

[131] (1431 – 1476) Called also *Vlad Draculea* (or *Dracula* by the foreigners, from The *Dragon* – knightly order he was member of) – Prince of Wallachia in 1448, 1456 – 1462 and 1476. The most famous of the Romanian rulers due the novel authored by Bram Stoker, *Dracula.*

[132] *Stephen III*, called *Stephen the Great* (1433 – 1504) – Prince of Moldova between 1457 and 1504. His reign had spanned 47 years, time interval never matched in the history of Moldova. During his tenure he fought battles against several of his neighbors, like the *Ottoman Empire, the Kingdom of Poland and the Kingdom of Hungary.* He was engaged in 42 battles and lost but 5! Churches and monasteries erected during his reign are today on the world heritage UNESCO list. He is regarded as a symbol of the struggle for independence of the Christians against the Ottoman expansion, being declared the greatest leader in the whole history of Romania.

[133] (1595 – 1661) – Prince of Moldova (1634 – 1653 and May 8, 1653 – July 16, 1653), dubbed *The Albanian* or *the Greek*.

[134] (1640 – 1688) – Prince of Wallachia between 1678 and 1688. Member of the illustrious Byzantine family of Cantacuzino, the son of the well known great boyar Constantine Cantacuzino and brother of the great scholar, the Stolnic Constantin Cantacuzino. As Prince of Wallachia, under Ottoman vassalage, he joined the Ottoman army besieging Vienna in 1683. But after talks with the Imperials Wallachia took the Christians side, aiming at the position of *Protector* of the Christians in the Balkan Peninsula, the Habsburgs promising him the imperial throne of a Constantinople freed from pagans (Muslims).

[135] (1654 – 1714) – Prince of Wallachia between 1688 and 1714, his reign being one of the longest in the history of the Romanian Principalities, nephew to the sister of Prince Serban Cantacuzino, he had inherited and enlarged a vast fortune consisting of real estates, personal properties and large amounts of money deposited abroad. During his tenure Wallachia had undergone a long period of peace, cultural flourishing and development of spiritual life, his leaving behind many religious institutions and an eclectic architectural style bearing his name.

[136] (in Ottoman Turkish *Devlet-i Aliye-i Osmaniye*, "The Sublime Ottoman State;" in modern Turkish: *Osmanlı Devleti* or *Osmanlı Imparatorluğu*, often named *Ottoman Turkey*, too) – imperial superpower that had dominated the Mediterranean Area between 1299 and 1922. In the beginning it had been a *Sunni* Islamic State founded by the Oghuz Turks under the rule of Osman I in north western Anatolia. It was also called *Sublime Porte*.

[137] (died 1685) – Prince of Moldova (September 1665 – May 1666; November 1668 – August 10, 1672; November 1678 – December 25, 1683) and *Walachia* (November/ December 1674 – November 1678). In 1680 the Turks appointed him Hetman of Ukraine.

[138] From Slavonic *stolu* "table" – boyar rank used in the Middle Age in the Romanian Provinces (Wallachia and Moldova), designating the court dignitary tending for the prince's table. During particular events or on holidays he was serving the prince, tasting the meals in front of him to prove they were not poisoned. His subalterns, *vtoristolnici* and *tretistolnici,* were serving the prince during usual meals while s*tolniceii*, some at the court and the others in the villages, were levying taxes for the fish caught in ponds and the Danube River. The Stolnic's subalterns made up a military category.

[139] The first *Prince's Court* from Bucharest (the capital city of the modern Romania), fallen in disrepair after the 1718 fire which burned to the ground the entire Bucharest, and

after the 1738 earthquake. The entire Prince‫s Court consisted of a palace – *The Voivode Palace*, and a church – *The Annunciation Church*, later known under the name *The Old Court Church*, guest hall houses, Prince‫s chancelleries, mews and gardens. There is little known about the founder of the court, but according to the researchers that had studied the history of Bucharest the court seems to have been built by Mircea the Elder in the late XIV century and early XV century. After the two calamities from XVIII century which had destroyed the court and the adjoining buildings, a new Prince‫s Court had been built, *The New Court.* In the present the ruins of the Voivode Palace became a protected archeological site, a museum having been also arranged, *The Old Court Museum.*

[140] Historical building in *Mogosoaia* locality, Ilfov County, Romania, about 15 kilometers away from Bucharest. The premises consists of the building itself, its court with the *watchtower*, *cuhnia* (kitchen), the *guesthouse*, the *ice cellar* and the vault of Bibescu family as well as the *Saint George Church* nearby the court walls. The palace bears the name of boyar Mogos, the owner of the land the palace had been erected on. Mogosoaia Palace was in the possession of Brancoveanu family for about 119 years, later on having been bought by Bibescu family.

[141] *Nicolae Milescu* or *Neculai Milescu Spatarul* (1636 – 1708) – Moldovan scholar, translator, traveler, geographer

and diplomat, active both in Moldova and the Russian Tsardom.

[142] (*Grigoras* or *Grigore Gheorghe Ghica*) – *Prince* of *Wallachia* two times: between September 1, 1660 – Nov. 1664 and February 1672 – November 1673.

[143] (died 1668), also called *Burduja* – Prince of Moldova between April 13, 1653 – May 8, 1653 and July 16, 1653 – March 13, 1658.

[144] Tsar from the Romanov dynasty (1645 – 1676).

[145] (About 1575 – 1620) – Prince of Moldova (1619 – 1620). Catholic Italian from Dalmatia, due to the war between Habsburgs and Ottomans had emigrated to Gradacz, on the shore of Lake Culpa. Mostly on the move, after working as servant several times, went to Venice. He was well read, having a good command of Italian, Croat, German, English and Turk. He learned English from the emissaries (ambassadors) of the King of England, Jacob I, Sir Henry Wotton and Sir Dudley Carleton. He travels to Constantinople with Sir Paul Pindar where he becomes firstly translator and then *dragoman*. Carrying out several missions and making friends at the Ottoman Court, the Italian Dragoman entertained hopes of being rewarded for his activity with the throne of a Romanian Province. On February 4, 1619 he became Prince of Moldova, being enthroned with a view to thwart the Kingdom of Poland's attempts to extend its borders over the Dniester River. Later

on he becomes a symbol of the fight against the Ottomans. Follower of the politics of *Michael the Brave*, the sole Romanian leader in history to have succeeded in 1600 in uniting all of the three Romanian medieval states (Wallachia, Moldova and Transylvania), he sought alliances with the Christians and fought the Ottomans, while further on uniting the Romanian Provinces. In the beginning he concluded an alliance with Poland, signing the treaty in the presence of Hetman Żółkiewski at Hotin. Getting wind of what happened in Iasi (the capital of Moldova at that time), the Sultan went swiftly into action. The Turks, headed by Skender-beg, Serakser of Caramania (Generalissimo of the Danube territories), and assisted by the Tatars led by Galga-sultan, Cantemir-bey and Aladin, had invaded Moldova. The Moldovan-Polish army had been defeated and the Prince fled the battlefield aiming to go to Transylvania, but was apprehended and beheaded.

[146] Word of Syriac or Akkadian origin (somehow related to the Arabian word *tarmunjan*) designating a position cumulating duties of translator, interpret and official guide in states and other political entities from Middle East. The status of a *dragoman* was in particular highly regarded within the Ottoman Empire, where the position was implying diplomatic attributes over the relations between the *High Porte* and the Christian States.

[147] *Austrian Empire* – (in German *Kaisertum Österreich*) former state formation in the Central Europe between 1804

and 1918. However, sometimes the name Austrian Empire is used in relation to earlier periods to designate thus the domains belonging to the House of Habsburg under which rule, *besides the Holy Roman Empire of the German Nation*, were also: Hungary, Croatia, Transylvania (1699), Galicia (1772), Bucovina (1775) and Dalmatia. The Empire had been officially proclaimed in 1804 on the basis of the crown domains of the Habsburg Family, in possession of the German imperial crown from XV century to the early XIX century.

[148] In Polish *Zygmunt III Waza* (1566 – 1632) – King of Poland and *Grand Duke* of Lithuania from 1587 until 1632 and monarch of Sweden from 1592 until 1599.

[149] Reference is made to *Stephen the Great*, Prince of Moldova, alleged to have been the defender of Christianity and Europe against the Turks and Islam. He was a *true athlete of the Christian faith*, as depicted by Pope Sixtus VI in a letter drawn up right during the wars Stephen the Great was waging against the Turks.

[150] Capital of Romania and at the same time the most populous city and the greatest industrial and commercial centre of the country. Its population of 1,883,425 inhabitants (2011) makes Bucharest the tenth most populous city in the European Union. According to some assessments Bucharest takes in every day over four million people. The first mention of the locality appears in 1459 during the reign of Vlad the Impaler. In 1862 it becomes the capital of the

United Principalities, undergoing later constant changes and turning into the Romanian cultural, artistic and media center. The fashionable architecture and the urban atmosphere brought it in the *Belle Époque* the surname *Little Paris*. Nowadays it is on administrative par with the Counties of Romania, being divided in six districts.

[151] *Iasi Municipality* (scholarly *Iasii* and *Targu Iesilor* respectively; historically *Jassy* or *Iassy*) – the residence of Iasi County and the main urban centre in North-Eastern Romania. Iasi had been the capital city of Moldova between 1564 and 1859, one of the two capitals of the United Principalities between 1859 and 1862, and capital of the Romanian Kingdom between 1916 and 1918. It is the fourth city in Romania by population and the cultural, economic and academic centre of Moldova. Here had been founded the still active *Alexandru Ioan Cuza University*, the oldest modern university in Romania, as well as other four public universities and seven private.

[152] *Wenzel Anton von Kaunitz* (1711 – 1794) – count, from 1764 imperial prince of Kaunitz – Rietberg, Austrian politician. In 1735 he entered state service, from 1750 until 1753 being ambassador of Austria to Paris. In 1753 he is appointed chancellor and likewise in charge of the imperial foreign policy.

[153] Born *Daniel Defoe* (1660 – 1731) – English journalist and writer. Famous through his novel Robinson Crusoe (1719), a narrative about a shipwrecked sailor who found himself

alone on an island. Along with Samuel Richardson, Defoe is deemed the father of the English novel and the first great realist novelist in the English literature.

[154] (In French: *Deuexieme Bureau*) – French intelligence agency founded by the ministry decision from February 29, 1920.

[155] *Secret Intelligence Service* (MI6) – is engaged in gathering information by way of human means, the espionage agency of Great Britain.

[156] *The Dreyfus Affair* had been a major political and social scandal during the Third French Republic, broken out in the late XIX century, about the treason charge directed against Captain Alfred Dreyfus, an Alsace origin French of Mosaic confession who in the end was exonerated. The affair had convulsed French society for twelve years, from 1894 until 1906, deeply dividing it in the long term between two opposing camps, the dreyfusards (supporting his innocence) and the anti-dreyfusards (supporting his guilt). The condemnation of Captain Dreyfus in the late XIX century for having supposedly passed on secret documents to the German Empire proved to be a miscarriage of justice against the background of espionage, in a social atmosphere fueling anti-Semitism and hate against the German Empire following the annexation of Alsace and parts of Lorene in 1871. The affair had triggered several political and social crises never seen before in France. The scandal came to a definitive conclusion only in 1906 through a decision of the

Cassation Court which had exonerated and definitively rehabilitated Dreyfus.

[157] *Frederick Louis, Prince of Wales* (1707 – 1751) – member of the *House of Hanover*, the first child of King George II and father of King George III of Great Britain and the great grandfather of Queen Victoria of United Kingdom.

[158] *François - Marie Arouet* (known as *Voltaire*) - (1694 – 1778) – writer and philosopher of the French Enlightenment.

[159] *Frederic II the Great*, in German *Friedrich II* (1712 – 1786) – King of Prussia (1740 – 1786), from Hohenzollern dynasty, the fourth prince-elector of the *Holy Roman Empire* under the name of *Frederick IV* (*Friedrich IV*) *of Brandenburg*. He became known under the name *Frederic the Great* (in German: *Friedrich der Große*), being dubbed *The Old Fritz* (in German: *Der Alte Fritz*).

[160] (1732 – 1799) – Both French and American watchmaker, inventor, musician, politician, refugee, spy, editor, arms smuggler and revolutionary. He made himself a name by way of his theatre plays, in particular the three plays on the *Figaro* barber.

[161] (1710 – 1774), called *The Much Beloved One* (in French: *le Bien-Aimé*) – King of France and Navarre (1715 – 1774).

[162] *Giacomo Girolamo Casanova de Seingalt* (1725 – 1798) – amorous Italian daredevil from Venice, famous through his

chivalrous adventures referred to in the *Memoires* ("The Story of my Life"), written between 1791 and 1798, comprising his adventurous life, convictions and experiences, standing out by a good knowledge and depiction of the mores of that time.

[163] (1757 – 1832) – French clergyman and politician.

[164] (1755 – 1824) – King of France and Navarre (1814 and 1815 – 1824).

[165] *Napoleon Bonaparte*, in French *Napoléon Bonaparte*, later known as *Napoleon I* and initially as *Napoleone di Bonaparte* (1769 – 1821) – political and military leader of France whose actions had heavily influenced the European policy in the early XIX century. Emperor of France and King of Italy. He went down in history as one of the great military strategists of the world and the creator of the *Napoleonic Code* that laid foundations to the judicial and administrative legislation of most of the Western Europe countries.

[166] (1754 – 1838) well known as Talleyrand – French diplomat and politician. From a high nobility family, he chose an ecclesiastical career upon the suggestion of his uncle, the Archbishop of Reims. He becomes priest and then Archbishop of Autun. During the French Revolution he relinquishes the clerical life and enters a layman⍰s one. He held various high offices of counselor, ambassador, foreign ministry, President of the Council of Ministers of France.

[167] (1840 – 1902) – French novelist, the most important representative of the naturalist school and a major figure of the French political liberation.

[168] *Otto Eduard Leopold von Bismarck - Graf von Bismarck* (in German: count) and *Fürst von Bismarck-Schönhausen* (in German: prince)/ (1815 – 1898) – Prussian/Germany statesman at the end of XIX century, as well as a commanding figure in world affairs. As Prime Minister (in German: *Ministerpräsident*) of Prussia between 1862 and 1890 he supervised the unification of Germany from 1870. In 1867 he is appointed chancellor of the *Northern Germany Confederation.* He devised the German Empire from 1871, becoming its first chancellor (*Chancellor of the Empire*) and in charge of its affairs until his removal from 1890. His diplomacy, known as real politics (*Realpolitik*) and the highhandedly manner of ruling the state brought him the nickname *the Iron Chancellor* (in German: *der Eiserne Kanzler*).

[169] (1741 – 1801) – firstly a rebel in the 13th colony on the eastern North-American coast, becoming later general in the *Continental Army.* He sided with the Englishmen, being seen as a traitor in the United States.

[170] (1732 – 1799) – American general and statesman, active militant in the North American colonies gaining independence from the United Kingdom, the first president of the United States of America.

[171] (1706 – 1790) – one of the most outstanding personalities in the history of the United States, one of the famous *Founding Fathers* of American nation, diplomat, scientist, inventor, philosopher, professor and politician.

[172] Known as *The Little Union* (*The Great Union* of Romania being that from 1918), had taken place at the middle of XIX century through the union of the Moldova and Wallachia states under the name *The United Principalities of Moldova and Wallachia.* The union was associated with the personality of Alexandru Ioan Cuza (see [175]) and his election as Ruler of both principalities on January 5, 1859 (Moldova) and January 24, 1859 (Wallachia).

[173] *Caimacamie* is a word coming from the modern term c*aimacam*, of Turkish origin, meaning *deputy*. The term caimacam originates from two Arabian words, namely *Kâim* and *Makâm.* It was used in Wallachia and Moldova since XVII century in the form *Caimacam Domnesc* (in Romanian). While waiting for or in the absence of the Ruler (in Romanian: *Domnitor*) usually two boyars were appointed to rule the princedom. From XIX century had been in use the designation *Locotenenta Domneasca* (Ruler Vice-regency). Under this name there are in particular known the 1856 vice-regencies, after the Rulers appointed for 7 years had stepped down, until the regulation of the *Danube Principalities* position in accordance with the new provisions of the Treaty of Paris. These vice-regencies instituted by the Ottoman

Empire were meant to overlook the elections for the ad-hoc reunions such as those standing against union prevail.

[174] Or *Vogoridis* or *Bogoridi*, (1820 – 1863) – *caimacam* (deputy, regent – see [173]) ruling Moldova between 1857 and 1858.

[175] Or *Alexandru Ioan I* (1820 – 1873) – the first Ruler of the *United Principalities* and the *Romanian National State*. He actively joined the 1848 revolutionary movement from Moldova and the struggle for the *Union of Principalities*. On January 5, 1859, Cuza had been elected Ruler of Moldova, and on January 24, 1859 of Wallachia, too, being thus accomplished the union of the two principalities. The full completion of the *Union of the Romanian Principalities*, in regard of a constitutional and administrative union, had been done in January 1862 when Moldova and Walachia had formed a unitary state, officially adopting the name Romania and making up the modern Romanian state with the capital at Bucharest, a single assembly and government. Cuza had been forced to abdicate in 1866 by a wide political alliance of that time, named the *Monstrous Coalition*, due to the divergent political allegiances of their members who had thus reacted to the authoritarian manifestations of the Romanian ruler.

[176] *The Romanian War of Independence* is the name used in the Romanian historiography to designate the participation of the *United Principalities* to the Russia-Turkey war from

1877 – 1878. In consequence of that war Romania had gained independence toward the Ottoman Empire.

[177] The peasant uprising (revolt) from 1907 (Romania) started off on February 21 in the Flamanzi village, Botosani County, and spread later on throughout the country. The uprising had been defeated by the government, the armed reprisal leaving in its wake the lives of many peasants (some historians put the figure of the victims among peasants to more than 40,000). The main reason was the peasants getting disgruntled with the unjust land ownership concentrated in the hands of few great proprietors.

[178] *Carol I of Romania, Prince of Hohenzollern-Sigmaringen*, under his full name *Karl Eitel Friedrich Zephyrinus Ludwig von Hohenzollern-Sigmaringen* (1839 – 1914) – Ruler then King of Romania who led the Romanian Principalities and later Romania after the forced abdication (through a coup d'état) of Alexandru Ioan Cuza.

[179] *Franz Joseph I of Austria* - in Romanian *Francisc Iosif I*, in German *Franz Josef I*, in Hungarian *Ferenc József I*, in Czech *František Josef I*, in Croat *Franjo Josip I*, in Italian *Francesco Giuseppe I* (1830 – 1916) – Emperor of Austria from the House of Habsburg, King of Hungary and Bohemia, King of Croatia, Great Duke of Bukovina, Great Prince of Transylvania, Marquis of Moravia, Great Voivode of the Voivodeship of Serbia – from 1848 until 1916.

[180] (1871 – 1955) – Romanian politician.

[181] *Military Intelligence, Section Five* (official name: *Security Service*) – British counter-information and home security. Along with *Secret Intelligence Service* (*SIS* or *MI6*), *Government Communications Headquarters* (*GCHQ*) and *Defense Intelligence Staff* (*DIS*) is part of *Joint Intelligence Committee* (*JIC*).

[182] *Grigori Yefimovich Rasputin* (1869 – 1916) – Russian peasant and mystic faith healer that bore a great influence on the family of the last Romanov tsar. Rasputin played a unique role in the life of Tsar Nicholas II, Tsarina Alexandra and their only son Tsarevitch Alexei, afflicted with hemophilia. Rasputin had been dubbed the *Mad Monk,* too, despite his having never taken the vow and coming out as married.

[183] (1888 – 1935), better known as *T. E. Lawrence* – British officer, famous in particular for the role played in the Arab uprising from 1916 – 1918, but whose lively personality and writings over a wide range of activities and associations led to him ending up as an object of fascination all over the world under the name *Lawrence of Arabia.*

[184] *Alexander Fyodorovich Kerensky* (1881 – 1970) – the second Prime Minister of the Russian Provisional Government, just before the Bolsheviks of Lenin had seized power.

[185] (1867 – 1933) – English novelist, Nobel Prize laureate for literature in 1932.

[186] (1965 – 1936) – famous British poet and novelist, Nobel Prize laureate for literature in 1907. Known mostly through his children story *Jungle Book* (1894), the Indian spy novel *Kim* (1901), poems *Gunga Din* (1892) and *If* (1895), and many other short stories and novellas. In 1934 he had been awarded, along with William Butler Yeats, *the Gothenburg Prize for Poetry*. During his life he was seen a great poet and offered a nobility title and position of *poet laureate* – which he both turned down.

[187] (1859 – 1930) – British novelist, famous for having created Sherlock Holmes – the first detective appearing in a series of whodunits. Besides these *Sir Arthur Conan Doyle* had authored many science fiction stories, period novels, theatre plays, romance novels, poems and non-fiction works.

[188] – In accordance with the original in French, *Légion d'honneur,* is the highest French civilian and military distinction, instituted in 1802 and awarded on and on from 1804 until the present days.

[189] – *Margaretha Geertruida Zelle* (1876 – 1917) – after an unfortunate marriage with a Dutch officer of English origin, Campbell MacLeord, she became renowned throughout Europe as dancer, courtesan and spy for Germany during the First World War. She was condemned and executed for espionage by a French firing squad on November 15, 1917.

[190] *The Battle of Marasesti* (August 6 – 19, 1917) – the most important military operation carried out by the Romanian

Army during the First World War against the German Troops. It was a complex operation aiming to defend and hold the frontline, interspersed with many Romanian offensive actions, against the background of a Russian army in utter revolutionary disarray.

[191] *John Griffith Chaney* (1876 – 1916) – American writer and journalist.

[192] *Eugen Berthold Friedrich Brecht* (1898 – 1956) – German playwright, poet and director, initially expressionist, founder of the theatrical institution *Berliner Ensemble*, creator of the epic theatre, he had promoted a new practice and theory of theatre based on epic distancing. He was one of those who had revolutionized the theatre of the XX century.

[193] *Paul Thomas Mann* (1875 – 1955) – German novelist, essayist, one of the greatest writers of the XX century, laureate of the Nobel Prize for literature in 1929 (the main reason being the novel *Buddenbrooks*).

[194] Known as Emperor *Shōwa* (1901 – 1989) – the 124th Emperor of Japan, the ruler with the longest reign on the throne of his country (62 years). He was the first monarch of the *Chrysanthemums Throne* who in 1946, after the defeat of his country in the Second World War had been forced to renounce the *divine right*. Under his rule Japan gained the status of great Asian power. *Shōwa* likewise represents the

name of the epoch he had ruled in, the longest of a Japan Emperor.

[195] In Chinese, literally *Manchu State*, in Japanese *Manshū-koku* or *Manchuria* – puppet state in Manchuria and eastern Inner Mongolia governed as a constitutional democracy. The region is the historical land of the Manchurian people which had founded the Chinese Dynasty *Quing*. In 1931, after the *Mukden Incident*, the region had been occupied by Japan while in 1932 there had been installed a pro Japanese government, *Puyi*, the *last Quing Emperor*, being appointed regent and emperor.

The Manchukuo government had been abolished in 1945 after the defeat of the Nippon Empire at the end of the Second World War. The territory belonging to the puppet state had been initially occupied by the soviet forces after the invasion of Manchuria from August 1945, it being transferred to the Chinese administration the following year.

[196] *Chiang Kai-shek* or *Jiang Jieshi* (1887 – 1975) – Chinese politician, leader of the national government from Nanjing (1928 – 1949). As leader of *Kuomintang* (nationalistic political movement, the first Chinese political party shaped by western standards, founded in 1921), he had contributed to the unification of China.

[197] *Jaime Ramón Mercader del Río* (1913 – 1978) – known mostly as Ramon Mercader, was a Spanish communist and KGB agent who had assassinated the Jewish origin Russian

revolutionary Marxist Leon Trotsky (1940) in Mexico. He served 20 years in a Mexican prison for first degree murder. Joseph Stalin awarded him the *Lenin Order* in absentia. Mercader was also awarded the title *Hero of the Soviet Union* after having been set free in 1961.

[198] *Leon Trotsky* (1879 – 1940), born *Lev Davidovich Bronstein*, Bolshevik revolutionary and Russian Marxist intellectual born in a family of Ashkenazi Jews from Ukraine. Important politician in the early Soviet Union, firstly *People's Commissary for Foreign Affairs*, and later on founder and first commander of the *Red Army* and *People's Commissary for Defense*. He was also founding member of *Politburo*. In consequence of his struggle for power with Joseph Stalin in the twenties, Trotsky had been removed from the Communist Party and exiled abroad. In the end he was assassinated in Mexico by a soviet agent. Trotsky's ideas underpin a communist theory known as *Trotskyism*.

[199] See [155]

[200] *Československo* in Czech, *Česko-Slovensko* in Slovak – Central European country between 1918 until December 31, 1992. On January 1, 1993, in accordance with a prior political decision of the Czechoslovakia Parliament it was divided into the Czech Republic and Slovak Republic following a peaceful political process known as the *Velvet Divorce*.

[201] French State (in French, *L'État Français*), known also as the *Vichy Regime* (in French, *Régime de Vichy*) – political regime of France from 1940 until 1944 instituted after Nazi Germany had defeated France and the *British Expeditionary Force* in the Battle of France during the Second World War. The Wehrmacht had taken over northern France, region under a lower authority of the Vichy Regime, its exerting a greater authority in the unoccupied southern France. However, in November 1942 the southern France had been also entirely subjected to the German government. The *Vichy Regime* was allied with the *Axis Powers*. It was the successor of the *Third French Republic*. The latter had been abolished on July 10, 1940, the new regime being instated over the main territory. That time the government had been sworn into office at Vichy, reason why we call it the *Vichy Government*. The *Constitutional acts* passed on July 11, 1940 by Senate and the Chamber of Deputies (convened in the Vichy Parliament) had instituted the *French State* in lieu of the *French Republic*. The laws enacted by the *Vichy Regime* had been nullified by a decree from August 9, 1944 which had restored the *Republic*.

[202] Lagoon harbor on Oahu Island, Hawaii, United States of America. Most of the harbor and the surrounding lands make up a United States naval base where is headquartered the *United States Pacific Fleet*. The Japanese attack on *Pearl Harbor* from December 7, 1941 had the United Stated enter into the Second World War. The attack, devised by Admiral

Yamamoto, had been inspired by the English attack on the Italian warships in Taranto harbor.

[203] *John Edgar Hoover* (1895 – 1972) – director of Federal Bureau of Investigation from May 10, 1924 until his death, namely for 48 years! As yet J. Edgar Hoover is the longest running head of an American agency, serving under eight presidents, from Calvin Coolidge to Richard Nixon. After him a ten years mandate for the position of FBI director had been instituted.

[204] In German: *Vergeltungswaffe 2* – Retribution Weapon 2, referred to in the Soviet/Russian literature as *Fau 2*, after the German pronunciation of letter "V", whose technical denomination is *Aggregat 4* (A-4), the first long range ballistic rocket developed during the Second World War in Germany, directly envisaged for use against London, and later Anvers. *V2* had been designed at the experimental station Peenemunde under the technical supervision of Wernher von Braun, and mass produced at *Mittelwerke* factory nearby Nordhausen in the south of Harz Mountains. Beginning with September 1944 more than 3,000 *V2* rockets had been launched by the German Wehrmacht against Allied targets during the war, most of them aimed at London, and then Anvers and Liege. The rocket had a 400 km range and moving at supersonic speed. The destructions it provoked were substantial. The attacks left in their wake about 9,000 military and civilian dead, while during the mass production of the weapon other 12,000 persons were believed to have

also died, subjected to hard labor and concentration camp prisoners.

[205] *Ian Lancaster Fleming* (1908 – 1964) – British writer and journalist, known for having created *James Bond* (007) whose adventures have been published in 12 novels and 2 short stories. Having sold about 100,000,000 copies all over the world, the books on the British spy made the list of the greatest bestsellers from all times. Fleming had been involved in the *Operation Goldeneye*. His military service during the war and the experience in journalism helped him creating the background and the details used in the James Bond series.

[206] *Henry Graham Greene* (1904 – 1991) – English writer, playwright, scenarist and literary critique.

[207] *Harold Adrian Russell "Kim" Philby* (1912 – 1988) – British double agent, high ranking member of the *Secret Intelligence Service* (*MI6*) who had spied for NKVD and KGB. In 1963 it had been found that Kim Philby was member of a spy ring known today as *Cambridge Five* or *Magnificent Five*, whose members, besides Philby, were: Donald Maclean, Guy Burgess, Anthony Blunt and John Cairncross. Between 1946 and 1965, when having been spying for the soviets, Kim Philby was officer of *The Order of the British Empire*.

[208] *Fidel Alejandro Castro Ruz* (n. 1926) – Cuban revolutionary who had participated in the overthrow of the Fulgencio Batista dictatorship and transforming Cuba into the first communist state of the Western Hemisphere. He held the office of Prime Minister until 1976, when he became chair of the *State Council* and *Council of Ministers.* Fidel Castro Ruz had been prime-secretary of the Cuban Communist Party (PCC) since its inception in 1965. His brother, Raul, succeeded Fidel Castro in 2008. Fidel Castro was one of the most hunted men in history with many failed attempts on his life carried out. Fabian Escalante, former head of the Cuban counter-information services charged with protecting Fidel Castro during his 49 years in office, had estimated 638 attempts at the life of Castro!

[209] Abbreviation from German of *Geheime Staatpolizei* – the official *Secret State Police* of Nazi Germany. GESTAPO it was subordinated to SS and administered by *Reichssicherheitshauptamt* (*RSHA*). Along with the intelligence agency *Sicherheitsdienst* had been incorporated into RSHA (*Department IV*). The Gestapo uniforms were black. In each concentration or extermination camp there was a Gestapo section called *Politische Abteilung* (political section). Run like an inquisitorial institution it was held responsible for the death of thousands of people. At the Nuremburg Trials it had been declared criminal organization by the allied military tribunals.

[210] *Freda Josephine McDonald* (1906 – 1975) – American origin French dancer, actress and singer. Born in Saint Louis, Missouri (USA) she joined the Second World War on the Allied side, assisting through spying actions the *French Resistance* led by Charles de Gaulle. She was the first American woman decorated with *Croix de Guerre* (The War Cross).

[211] *Theodore Herman Albert Dreiser* (1871 – 1945) – American naturalist writer known by the manner he was approaching the reality of life in his work.

[212] *Charles (Charlie) Spencer Chaplin* (1889 – 1977) – English actor and director. He is deemed as one of the greatest cinema stars from XX century. The most renowned feature movies of his are *City Lights, Modern Times* and *The Dictator.*

[213] *Walter Elias Disney* (1901 – 1966) – American director, producer, animator, scenarist and entrepreneur, 22 times winner of the Oscar Awards. He is a household name in America, being known even by the kids.

[214] *Anton Pavlovich Chekhov* (1860 – 1904) – Russian physician, novelist and playwright.

[215] *Eva Anna Paula Hitler*, born *Braun* (1912 – 1945) – she had been for 14 years Hitler's mistress and in her last 36 hours of life his wife. Unassuming and properly raised, she was a middle class young woman harboring no anti-Semitic feelings, who had never joined the Nazi Party. For the sake

of her *Fuhrer* she forwent everything meaningful in her life (marriage, children, her own home, pride and the assent of her parents). The data on this woman are scanty. Hitler▢s henchmen paid her no attention, and the wives of high ranking Nazi officials barely stood her. In June 1944 the English secret services still believed she was but the Fuhrer▢s secretary. In April 1945, while the soviet army was fighting hard its way through a Berlin lying in ruins after relentless bombardments, she committed suicide along with Hitler in his bunker. Though having been his mistress for 14 years few knew her by name and appearance, Hitler succeeding so well in keeping her out of the public eye that she lived and died anonymously.

[216] *Hermann Wilhelm Goring*, often only *Hermann Goring* or *Hermann Goering*, (1893 – 1946) – German military pilot, politician, military commander, second on the National Socialist (Nazi) Party and the Third Reich hierarchy, after Adolf Hitler, and commander in chief of the Luftwaffe. The establishing of the first Hitlerite Germany concentration camps (prison like) and Gestapo (the State Secret Police) are closely tied to Goring. The tank division *Hermann Goring Panzerdivision* (armored and paratrooper division) which fought in Africa and Sicily, bore his name.

[217] *Lavrentiy Pavlovich Beria*, in Georgian: *Lavrenti Pavles dze Beria* (1899 – 1953) – soviet politician and chief of the secret police apparatus during Stalin▢s regime. Beria went down in history mainly as executor of the Stalinist purges in

the fourth decade of XX century, though involved only in its final stages. He participated in the Katyn massacre when about 22,000 Polish officers had been assassinated. Beria was a powerful figure during the Second World War and in the first months after the death of Stalin (short period where as vice-president minister he initiated a modest liberalization). In June 1953 he was charged with several crimes, and in December 23, 1945 was put on trial, sentenced to death and shot.

[218] *Karl Heinrich Marx*, born *Moses Mordecai Levi Marx* (1818 – 1883) – philosopher, historian, economist, sociologist and journalist, the founder, along with Friedrich Engels, of the *scientific socialism* theory, theoretician and leader of the workers movement.

[219] In original *Das Eiserne Kreuz* (EK) – military decoration of the Prussian Kingdom and then Germany⬚s, in the time of the Prussian King Frederick Wilhelm III, who instituted it on May 10, 1813. This decoration continues to be used in the present, too, an official German distinction awarded to military personnel during war.

[220] From the Russian language: *Kommunisticeskii internaţional – Communist International,* known as the *Third International* – communist international organization established in 1929 by Lenin and the Russian (Bolshevik) Communist Party having as objective *the fight through all possible means, armed struggle included, for overthrowing the global bourgeoisie and founding an international soviet*

republic as a transitional stage toward the definitive abolition of the state. Comintern had represented a scission of the left elements in the *Second International* in reaction to the latter's incapacity to set up a sound coalition against the First World War which the *Third International* deemed as imperialist war. Comintern held seven congresses, the first in March 1919 and the last in 1935. The groups affiliated to the left communism acknowledge today the validity of but the first two congresses, those of the Bolshevik, Leninist and Trotskyist tradition – only of the first four, while the Stalinist and Maoist parties of all the seven congresses.

[221] (1900 – 1945) – Nazi Germany politician, brought to trial at Nuremberg and sentenced to death *in absentia* for war crimes and crimes against humanity. Prior to the death of Hitler, *Martin Bormann* had been designated to succeed him at the leadership of the German National Socialist Workers Party. His skeleton had been found, identified, being established his having poisoned himself in Berlin in May 1945. His earthly remains had been burned and scattered over the Baltic Sea.

[222] *Ernest Miller Hemingway* (1899 – 1961) – novelist, war correspondent, Pulitzer Prize laureate (1953) Nobel Prize for Literature laureate (1954), one of the best known American writers in the world.

[223] (1893 – 1969) – American lawyer and diplomat, the first civilian to be appointed Director of the *Central Intelligence Agency* (CIA) and the person to have held that position the

longest. As CIA Director he personally overlooked the coup d'état in Guatemala, *Operation Ajax* (overthrowing the elected government of Iran), the development and building program of the spy planes *U2* and the *Bay of Pigs* invasion. Following the assassination of President John F. Kennedy, *Dulles* had been appointed member of the *Warren Commission*. Besides his governmental employment Dulles worked as lawyer and partner for *Sullivan & Cromwell*. His older brother, John Foster Dulles had been state secretary during the Eisenhower administration.

[224] Document whereby *The United Nation Organization* (founded in 1945 and having in the present 194 member states) is commissioned to provide *world peace, observance of the human rights, international cooperation and observance of the international law.* The document is the founding act of *UN.*

[225] *Franklin Delano Roosevelt* (1882 – 1945) – the 32th president of the United States of America (1933 – 1945). He stood out as one of the main political leaders of the XX century both at home and abroad, having an essential contribution to overcoming the international economic crisis and defeating Nazi Germany during the Second World War. He is also the only president in the history of the United States who had executed four mandates on end.

[226] *Reinhard Tristan Eugen Heydrich* (1904 – 1942) – high ranking Nazi Germany official, important member of NSDAP, SS *Obergruppenfuhrer* and Chief of Police, since

1939 head of the *Reich Main Security Office* (RSHA) subordinating Gestapo (secret police), *Sicherheitsdienst* (Security Service) and Criminal Police (*Kriminalpolizei*). He was also Reich Protector (*Reichprotektor*) of the so called *Protectorate of Bohemia and Moravia.* Hitler was seeing him as a possible successor of his. He was deemed by some as number three in the Nazi Germany hierarchy. Heydrich died of septicemia eight days after the attempt from May 27, 1942, where two Czech partisan agents airdropped by RAF had detonated an explosive which wrecked the car Heydrich was using to go in the morning to his office in Prague. As reprisals for the attempt Nazis had destroyed the Czech localities Lidice and Ležáky and exterminated their inhabitants. Over 13,000 Czechs had been arrested, deported, interned in concentration camps or killed.

[227] (1901 – 1992) – actress and singer. She is the first German actress to reach celebrity in Hollywood. Cabaret singer, choir girl and German movie actress in Berlin in the twenties, Hollywood star in the thirties and in the end internationally acclaimed figure, one of the idols of the XX century. In 1939, *Dietrich* had been granted US citizenship.

[228] *George Catlett Marshall,* known mostly as *George Marshall* (1880 – 1959) – American general, diplomat and politician laureate of the *Nobel Prize for P*eace.

[229] (1873 – 1953) – Romanian politician, Romanian deputy of Transylvania to the Parliament in Budapest, several times prime minister of Romania, head of the National Peasant

Party (government party), political detainee after 1947, dead in the communist prison at Sighet.

[230] *Ion Victor Antonescu*, known as *Marshall Antonescu* (1882 – 1946) – Romanian military and statesman, career officer, general, chief of the operation office of the *Romanian Army General Headquarters* in the First World War (when he directly defeated Lieutenant Erwin Rommel, that to become later the *Desert Fox* and Marshall of the *Third Reich*), military attaché to London and Paris, commander of the *High School of War*, *Chief of the General Headquarters* and war ministry, and from September 4, 1940 until August 23, 1944 Prime Minister of Romania and *Leader of the State*. He was removed from the state leadership by King Michael I through the coup d'état from August 23, 1944, being arrested and handed over to the communists, then detained in the Soviet Union. On May 17, 1946 he was sentenced to death for war crimes in a show trial set up by the Bolsheviks and held into the so called *People*s Tribunal* from Bucharest. On June 1, 1946 he was put to death by firing squad at Jilava Prison (nearby the Romanian capital, Bucharest).

[231] *General Inspectorate of the Romanian Gendarmerie* (*IGJR*) – military structure commissioned to maintain and restore public order, transport and guard valuables, goods and dangerous materials, as well as to protect and defend highly important objectives. The Romanian Gendarmerie is subordinated to the Internal Affairs Ministry. It was

established by an *Ofis domnesc* (in Romanian), document signed by the head of the Principality, issued on April 3, 1850 by the Prince of Moldova (Romanian historical region) Grigore Alexandru Ghica.

[232] (born 1921) – former King of Romania between July 20, 1927 and June 8, 1930, as well as between September 6, 1940 and December 30, 1947. He is one of the few World War Two leaders still alive. Son of the heir prince Carol, *Michael I* had inherited by birth the titles *Prince of Romania* and *Prince of Hohenzollern-Sigmaringen* (which he forwent later).

[233] (1913 – 1963) – Romania singer of popular, gypsy and romance music and music hall actress. She was dubbed *The Nightingale, Masterly Bird* and the *Queen of the Romanian Song.*

[234] (1895 – 1950) – former head of the *Romanian Special Intelligence Service* (secret services) between November 12, 1940 and March 1, 1945.

[235] known as *Princess Catherine Olympia Caradja,* born *Ecaterina Olimpia Cretulescu* (1893 – 1993) – Romanian aristocrat and philanthropist settled in the United States of America. Born in Bucharest, raised in England and France, she made it over the Romanian border in 1952, shaking off the communist regime aboard a small boat she crossed the Danube in to the then Yugoslavia. As expat to the United States for more than 35 years she had lived in the Hill

County, Texas wherefrom she returned to Romania after 1989 to live in Bucharest, where she died as centenarian at the patriarchal age of 100.

[236] *Secret Information Service* (mostly the *State Security/ Security*) – denomination the secret service of Romania had activated under until November 13, 1940, the name being later changed into *Special Information Service* (*SSI*).

[237] Pseudonym of *Jacques Forment*, French nationality Belgian writer and historian, worldwide renowned specialist on contemporary history, mostly preoccupied in the second world war. He was general secretary of the International Commission for History Learning.

REFERENCES

[I-VI] Popescu, Alexander, "From the Universal History of Espionage", article run into the printed edition of "ZIARUL FINANCIAR", April 21, 2011

[VII] Cerneak, E., "Five Centuries of Secret War" 1968, pp. 8-9

[VIII-XI] Popescu instead. cit., "From the Universal History…"

[XII] Cerneak, op. cit., p. 8

[XIII] Popescu instead. cit., "From the Universal History…"

[XIV] Cerneak, op. cit., p.10

[XV-XVIII] Popescu instead. cit., "From the Universal History…"

[XIX-XXV] Popescu, Alexander, "From the Universal History of Espionage", article run into the printed edition of "ZIARUL FINANCIAR", April 29, 2011

[XXVI-XXXIII] Ibid., May 6, 2011

[XXXIV-XXXVI] Ibid., May 13, 2011

[XXXVII-XLVIII] Ibid., June 10, 2011

[XLIX-LV] Ibid., June 17, 2011

[LVI-LXV] Ibid., June 24, 2011

[LXVI-LXXI] Ibid., July 1, 2011

* Author's note: The famous historian Mackinder wrote: "Up there, in the Romanian Maramures, there is a place marked as the centre of the Old Continent (Europe from Atlantic to Urals). Anyone leading Eastern Europe leads the core of Europe; that who leads the core of Europe leads the World Island; that who leads the World Island leads the World."

** Author's note: In a historical interpretation, Eastern Europe is the Old Europe, in the West life being possible only several millennia later. Westerners are descendants of the Easterners who migrated to the west in the IV millennium BC. This upturning of the historical truth belongs to Donald Rumsfeld, US secretary for defense, on an irked retort to France and Germany which were criticizing the occupation of Iraq (2003).

*** Author's note: The explanatory notes comprise data in historical archives as well as information from "Wikipedia, the free encyclopedia" part of "Wikimedia Foundation."

SELECTIVE BIBLIOGRAPHY

CAMACHO, Santiago, *Illuminati Conspiracy*, Media Group "LA ESFERA DE LOS LIBROS," Madrid, 2006

CERNEAK, E., *Five Centuries of Secret War*, POLITIC Publishing House, Bucharest, 1968

CHAMBERS, Whittaker, *Witness*, RANDOM HOUSE, New York, 1952

DEAKIN, F. W.; STORRY, G. R., *The Case of Richard Sorge*, HARPER AND ROW Publishing House, New York, 2011

DE LAUNAY, Jaques; GHEYSENS, Roger, *Les grands espions de notre temps*, HACHETTE, Paris, 1971

DOLOGA, Laurentiu, *Hitler☐s secret plan to smash the British economy*, ZIARE.COM, April 2, 2012

ESTULIN, Daniel, *The real history of the Bilderberg Club*, PLANETA Publishing House, Barcelona, 2005

ESTULIN, Daniel, *The Secrets of the Bilderberg Club*, PLANETA Publishing House, Barcelona, 2007

FALIGOT, Roger; KAUFFER, Remi, *Les maitres espions*, ROBERT LAFFONT, 1994

GANNON, John*, *CIA and the New World Order – challenges until 2015* (*GANNON, John had headed the National Information Council of USA – author☐s note)

GARZ, Florian, *Total Espionage in Action*, OBIECTIV Publishing House, Craiova, 2009

HAYNES, John Earl; KLEHR, Harvey, *Venona: Decoding Soviet Espionage in America*, CT: YALE UNIVERSITY PRESS, 1999

HAYNES, John Earl; KLEHR, Harvey; VASSILIEV, Alexander, *Spies: The Rise and Fall of the KGB in America*, New Haven, CT: YALE UNIVERSITY PRESS, 2009

HASWELL, J., *Spies and Spymaster - A Concise History of Intelligence*, London, 1977

HELM, Sarah, *The Secrets of Vera Atkins – The Story of a Romanian Woman Spy in the Second World War*, LITERA Publishing House, Bucharest, 2014

ICKE, David, *The Greatest Secret: The Book to Change the World*, Second edition, DAVID ICKE BOOKS, London, 1999

IOAN, Paul, *Stalin⬛s Golden Spy*, MAGAZIN, May 3, 2012

KOCH, Paul H., *Illuminati: Secrets and Conspirations*, PLANETA Publishing House, Barcelona, 2005

KOCH, Paul H., *The Occult History of the World*, BRONCE Publishing House, Barcelona, 2007

KNIGHTLEY, Philip, *The Master Spy*, KNOPF, New York, 1989

KNOLL, Reinholdt; HAIDINGER, Martin, *Spione, Spitzel und Agenten. Analyse einer Schattenwelt*, NP BUCHVERLAG, Viena, 2001

LUPSOR, Andreea, *A Look into the British Espionage through the Diaries of an MI5 Director*, HISTORIA Magazine

LLOYD, Mark, *The Guinness Book of Espionage*, GUINNESS Publishing House, London, 1994

MIHAI, Ioana, *The Secret Missions of a Soviet Spymaster*, BUSINESS MAGAZIN, March 29, 2013

POPESCU, Alexandru, "From the Universal History of Espionage," article run into the printed edition of ZIARUL FINANCIAR, 2011

POPESCU, Alexandru, *Five Millennia of Secret War – An encyclopedia of Espionage*, CETATEA DE SCAUN Publishing House, Targovişte, 2012

POPESCU, Alexandru, *The Secret Biographies of Spies – The Personal Life of the Agents*, CETATEA DE SCAUN Publishing House, Targovişte, 2014

PAPADIE, Bogdan A.; NĂSTASE, Gabriel I., *The Spy War*, First edition, PHOBOS Publishing House, 2005

PAPADIE, Bogdan A.; NĂSTASE, Gabriel I., *The Spy War*, Second edition, PHOBOS Publishing House, 2005

PAPADIE, Bogdan A.; NASTASE, Gabriel I., *Armageddon Romania*, volume I, OBIECTIV Publishing House, Craiova, 2012

PAPADIE, Bogdan A.; NASTASE, Gabriel I., *Armageddon Romania*, volume II, OBIECTIV Publishing House, Craiova, 2012

PAPADIE, Bogdan A.; NASTASE, Gabriel I., *Spies and the Revolution Coup d'état*, OBIECTIV Publishing House, Craiova, 2014

PARLOG, Nicu, "Richard Sorge – The Spy of the XX Century," DESCOPERA Publication, June 28, 2011

ROBERTSON, Pat, *The New World Order*, W. PUBLISHING GROUP, Irving - Texas, 1992

ROBERTS, Sam, *Figure in Rosenberg Case Admits to Soviet Spying*, in: THE NEW YORK TIMES, September 12, 2008

ROSETI, Roxana, *The Uncrowned Queen of Soviet Espionage*, 2004

SKARTSIUNI, Dimitriu, *Prophecies about Antichrist*, DESCOVERIES Collection, Athens, 1991

STEVENSON, William, *Vera Atkins. The Story of the most Important Secret Agent of Romanian Origin from the Second World War*, POLIROM Publishing House, Bucharest, 2014. Translated by SIULEA Ciprian

TRONCOTA, Cristian, *The History of the Romanian Secret Services. From Cuza to Ceauşescu*, ION CRISTOIU Publishing House, Bucharest, 1999

TANASE, Eugenia, *The Fair Sex in Cold Blood: Female Top Assassins and Spies*, FEMINIS.RO, March 27, 2013

WEINSTEIN, Allen; VASSILIEV, Alexander, *The Haunted Wood: Soviet Espionage in America – the Stalin Era*, RANDOM HOUSE, New York, 1999

Amy Elizabeth Thorpe: WWII's Mata Hari, HISTORYNET.COM, June 12, 2006